How to Interpret Your DNA Test Results For Family History & Ancestry

How to Interpret Your DNA Test Results For Family History & Ancestry

Scientists Speak Out on Genealogy Joining Genetics

Anne Hart

Writers Club Press
New York Lincoln Shanghai

How to Interpret Your DNA Test Results
For Family History & Ancestry
Scientists Speak Out on Genealogy Joining Genetics

All Rights Reserved © 2002 by Anne Hart

No part of this book may be reproduced or transmitted in any form or by any means, graphic, electronic, or mechanical, including photocopying, recording, taping, or by any information storage retrieval system, without the written permission of the publisher.

Writers Club Press
an imprint of iUniverse, Inc.

For information address:
iUniverse
2021 Pine Lake Road, Suite 100
Lincoln, NE 68512
www.iuniverse.com

ISBN: 0-595-26334-8

Printed in the United States of America

"For what is the worth of human life, unless it is woven into the life of our ancestors by the records of history?"—**Cicero**, ancient Rome's finest orator and rhetorician, (103–43 B.C.E). During the times of Spartacus and slave rebellions, Cicero presided over Roman law and politics for almost half a century.

Contents

Introduction ix
Chapter One Oral History Joins the Molecular Revolution 1
Chapter Two Personalizing Family History Records
             with DNA Testing 31
Chapter Three The Phenomics Revolution: My Positive Experiences
               with DNA Testing in My Genealogy Search
               and How This Information Helped Me Write
               My DNA Detective Novels 44
Chapter Four Companies That Bring the Power of DNA
              Technology to Your Home 69
Chapter Five What is DNA? 76
Chapter Six Human Genome Project 80
Chapter Seven What We've Learned So Far 86
Chapter Eight After the Human Genome Project (HGP),
               the Next Steps… 92
Chapter Nine How to Interview Older Adults for
              Intergenerational Writing about their Genealogy
              and Memories 99
Chapter Ten Diaries Plus DNA 127
Chapter Eleven Mapping Your Personal Anthropology with
                Genetic Genealogy 137
Chapter Twelve Managing a Genetic Genealogy Project:
                Participants with Poor Documentation 148
Chapter Thirteen Haplogroups and Markers 151
Chapter Fourteen Have a Personal or Family History of Cancer?
                  Consider Joining the Cancer Genetics Network ..160
Chapter Fifteen Dictionary of Genetic Terms 170
Appendix A 221
Appendix B: 225

Appendix C: 229
Appendix D 237
Index 239

INTRODUCTION

How do you interpret your own DNA test results? How do you write, tape, and transcribe an oral history? Assuming you're a beginner in genealogy with no science background and interested in family history, where do you begin your search? What's the cultural component behind a trait as biological as your genes? If you're a family historian, an oral history researcher, or a person fascinated with ancestry, here's how to understand the results of DNA tests.

Different people have different, sometimes opposite opinions on whether DNA testing is a useful tool in the hands of family historians. If you are a carrier of a genetic disorder, DNA testing is useful in researching your family history to find out who was the first carrier in your ancestry back in time.

Here the debate unfolds as scientists, authors, physicians, media people, owners of DNA testing companies, genealogists, historians and researchers comment, write, and opine on DNA testing and genealogy. How do you use DNA testing to interpret family history records? How eager are people to take a DNA test for family history research? Most DNA tests require only that someone swish mouthwash around in his or her mouth and send it for testing to a laboratory. So what can a DNA test really tell you about your own ancestry—distant or not so distant? And most of all, how do you interpret and use the results?

Here's a letter from Dr. Mark Humphrys:
Lecturer
School of Computer Applications,
Dublin City University,
Glasnevin, Dublin 9, Ireland.

"Dear Anne:

Here's a summary of the position as I see it:

Why everybody in the west is descended from Charlemagne:

We all know that all humans are related. So a good question is: When was our Most Recent Common Ancestor (MRCA)?

Surprisingly, the answer to that question is a lot more recent than DNA studies would suggest, since we are searching *all* lines of descent, rather than just the lines genes traveled on. You do not inherit *all* your ancestor's DNA, but only a small part of it. And yet, even if you inherit NONE of their DNA (which is not only possible, but *probable*, as you go back far enough), they are still your ancestor.

To find the answer to the MRCA, we need to look beyond DNA studies. Mathematical models suggest that, if humans picked mates randomly, the MRCA is in historical times, perhaps c. 1200 AD! This is an amazing result, suggesting that we do not have to go back into prehistory to find an ancestor of every single human! But obviously humans do not pick mates randomly—they tend to mate with people in their local geographic area.

Computer simulations that take this into account suggest that even with a high degree of local mating, the MRCA is still in historical times, perhaps c. 300 AD. If we consider just the West, the MRCA may be as recent as c. 1000 AD.

How realistic are these models?
Well, there has been a growing collection of REAL, proven descents from medieval figures in genealogy. For instance, my own children have proven descents—through many different lines—from Charlemagne, who lived around 800 AD. He is the ancestor of most of the royal houses of Europe and so is a natural focal point for the genealogies of the West.

My web page, Royal Descents of Famous People, is a large and growing list of famous people in the west who are all proven descendants of Charlemagne. And if all these people have proven descents, every step of the way, how many more people must have descents in reality that cannot be proved because of the scarcity of records? It must be a much greater number. My work is a strong indicator that *everyone* in the West descends from medieval royalty.

In short, work by a number of people—my genealogical study, other people's computer simulations and mathematical models—all confirm each other's findings that the MRCA for a large, interbreeding area such as the West, is within recent recorded history. Another finding of those models is that not long before the MRCA, if someone is the ancestor of *anyone* alive today, they are the ancestor of *all* people alive today. Since Charlemagne is probably around that early date for the West, and since he is a proven ancestor of *some* people, it is likely that he is the ancestor of *all* people in the West.

Everybody in the West is descended from Charlemagne:

In conclusion, if you have west European ancestry at all, it seems virtually impossible for you not to be descended from Charlemagne, who lived around 800 AD. 90 percent of the world (including all the West) is descended from Confucius:

For the MRCA of the whole world, we need to consider extremely isolate daboriginal populations. If they were truly isolated, we may have to go back thousands of years to get a common ancestor with them. For people who did not live in isolated enclaves though—the West, Middle East, more or less all of Asia, most of Africa—the MRCA is highly likely to be in recent historical times (late BC, possibly even AD). Anyone with ancestry from these areas is, for example, almost certainly a descendant of Confucius, who lived around 500 BC and who is a proven ancestor of *some* people alive today in China, hence probably ancestor of *all* people in the world except the extremely isolated.

This exciting consensus is fairly new, and is supported by three independent fieldsof (a) genealogy, (b) mathematical models, and (c) computer simulations.

The findings are robust with respect to barriers such as religion, class difference, etc.All one needs is a *tiny* amount of crossing of such barriers in the population in the past in order to get everyone today (of different religions etc.) with a recent common ancestor.

The only thing that can push back the MRCA before historical times is *total* geographic isolation of populations from each other, which we know did not happen for most of the world.

People are inspired (rightly so) by DNA studies of ancient common human ancestors tens of thousands of years ago. And yet the fact is that we are almost certainly *all* descended from any historical figure in classical times that left descendants."

-----
end quote

Web pages on MRCAs:
http://computing.dcu.ie/~humphrys/FamTree/Royal/ca.html
http://computing.dcu.ie/~humphrys/FamTree/Royal/ca.genetic.html
http://computing.dcu.ie/~humphrys/FamTree/Royal/ca.math.html
http://computing.dcu.ie/~humphrys/FamTree/Royal/famous.descents.html

The Web pages include a fantastic computer simulation by a gentleman named Rohde at MIT to work out the MRCA for a non-random mating model. He confirms much of Chang's work, and in general it is another strong indicator that the MRCA for the world (or 99 percent of it) is post-1000 BC—maybe even AD.

Regards
—Mark

Dr. Mark Humphrys
Lecturer
School of Computer Applications,
Dublin City University,
Glasnevin, Dublin 9, Ireland.
http://computing.dcu.ie/~humphrys/

CHAPTER ONE

Ask "Who We Are" of Your Family Member's DNA Sequences and Memorabilia and Show "Who We Were" in a Multimedia Scrapbook

Oral History Joins the Molecular Revolution

Steve Olson, author of the book, *Mapping Human History* in a telephone interview with me on December 3, 2002 at 1:50 PM EST answered my question—What do you say about using DNA as a tool for genealogy—to extend family history research?

"The most valuable use of DNA testing is to demonstrate how closely related we are to each other, both as individuals and as members of human groups," Steve Olson says. "I'm a skeptic about the *Seven Daughters of Eve* (book) because I believe that everyone in the world is descended from all seven of those women. As I point out in my book, *Mapping Human History.*

"As I point out in the book, I believe that everyone living today is descended from most people who lived a few millennia ago," Olson explains. "So genetic tests need to be interpreted very carefully or you draw false conclusions about being descended from a relatively small number of people."

Does Steve Olson think DNA testing as a tool is useful to genealogists? "No, I don't feel DNA testing can tell you things that can't be discovered in other ways. I should probably say here, though, that I'm fairly skeptical about DNA testing for genealogical purposes, and I'm particularly critical of the *Seven Daughters of Eve* idea."

The Seven Daughters of Eve is a book written by Bryan Sykes, from Oxford Ancestors. Bryan Sykes, MA PhD DSc, is Professor of Human Genetics, University of Oxford, and with Oxford Ancestors, who comments in chapter three of this book. Sykes has a different opinion about DNA testing and genealogy/family history research.

Oxford Ancestors is the world's first company to harness the power and precision of modern DNA-based genetics for use in genealogy. The motto on the Oxford Ancestors Web site at: <http://www.oxfordancestors.com/> reads: "Putting the genes in genealogy."

Oxford ancestors is based on more than a decade of research into human populations and their origins carried out by Professor Bryan Sykes, Professor of Human Genetics at the University of Oxford and his team in the world-renowned Institute of Molecular Medicine in Oxford, England. So as you read in this book, and any other books you research, there are many different experts in genetics, medicine, and the media with different opinions.

Science is supposed to be skeptical by nature as well as open-minded for change. Facts provide an open door to further inquiry, and facts need to be checked as new information comes in. So what stance will you take? Will you take the skeptical side on DNA testing? Or do you reason that DNA testing is one more tool that adds genes to genealogy? Where will you stand in this debate—observer, skeptic, or DNA researcher working with genealogy and genetics?

Perhaps you're a genealogist or oral historian doing family history research and you have no science background in genetics. Now that the molecular revolution has introduced DNA testing for ancestry research, here's how to use your curiosity. Perhaps you want to find information about tests of racial percentages or DNA testing and ancestry. Make up your own mind. Now you can combine DNA research and oral history research into one archive. How do you interpret DNA tests and how do you plan, record, and transcribe an oral history for your family or others?

DNA testing for ancestry is offered by companies that combine DNA testing (done by commercial laboratories and/or university laboratories) with surname genealogy. Various surname groups on the Web also offer discounts with DNA testing companies and laboratories. Ask for the facts.

Whom do you go to first, assuming you have no background in either science or genealogy? Scientists? The media? DNA testing companies? University laboratories? Oral historians? Genealogists? Biological anthropologists? DNA mailing lists on the Web? Whom can you trust? And where does the truth lie—in technology? It's like twelve blind men asked to describe an elephant. Each touches a different part of its body and replies, "it's a tail," or "it's a trunk." Everyone has a different opinion of the value of DNA testing in researching family history or ancestry. What do the changing scientific facts say, for now?

Question authority, and do your research. Then decide what tools are the best for you in your own family history quest. Perhaps you want to find out the percentage of various races in your ancestry. How do know where to begin your journey into the past and future? What if you're a foundling, an orphan, or have no knowledge of your own ethnicity? Can a DNA test at least tell you how many races are in your recent or ancient past? What facts do genetic markers really tell you about ancestry?

If you want to start your ancestry search with DNA testing, first you take the DNA tests along with tests of racial percentages if you desire. Even your DNA has a cultural component to its molecular biology. Then you interpret the results making the complex easy to understand for yourself or your clients. Your DNA testing service can help you find answers. So can many Web sites as well as this book and other books recommended here.

Next in your family history search, you collect letters, diaries, oral history transcriptions, home sources, artifacts, memorabilia, census research, wills-and-probate records, medical histories, land records, slave ownership records, if it applies to your or your client. Pay particular attention to social histories to fill some gaps left by lack of women's records.

Search through church, synagogue, mosque, pagoda, or temple records, vital records from the US government such as military records, social security information, and government pensions for retired government employees, employment and tax records, if any exist and are available. Check school records from elementary through college, if any, social histories, ethnic histories, and religious school records. Go to the family history Web sites, the ships' passenger lists. I highly recommend a book for searching women's ancestry, titled, *Discovering Your Female Ancestors*, by Sharon DeBartolo Carmack, Betterway Books, Ohio 1998, ISBN # 1-55870-472-8. The book's subtitle emphasizes "*Special strategies for uncovering hard-to-find information about your female lineage.*"

Marriage records often were in different languages representing the former country or languages of the ethnic group. You may need to translate a different alphabet to find a maiden name on a marriage certificate never registered, but obtained from clergy.

Then you review and analyze the records. Study the social history of the times and location of this individual. Add family history and migrations to social history, and you have the beginnings of an outline to write a biography of the ancestor as a family history.

Learn to interpret the results of your own DNA test and expand your historical research ability to trace your ancestry. "An interesting idea was expressed by a colleague from Canada, Dr. Charles Scriver," explains geneticist, Dr. Batsheva Bonné-Temir. "At a meeting which I organized here in Israel on **Genetic Diversity Among Jews** in 1990, Dr. Scriver gave a paper on '*What Are Genes Like that Doing in a Place Like This? Human History and Molecular Prosopography*.' He claimed that a biological trait has two histories, a biological component and a cultural component." Dr. Charles Scriver is founder of the DeBelle Laboratory of Biochemical Genetics in Canada. He also established screening programs in Montreal for thalassaemia and Tay Sachs Disease.

According to Bonné-Tamir, at the 1990 meeting in Israel on *Genetic Diversity Among Jews*, Dr. Charles Scriver stated, "When the event clusters and an important cause of it is biological, the cultural history also is likely to be important because it may explain why the persons carrying the gene are in the particular place at the time."

The term, "when the event clusters" refers to an event when genes cluster together in a DNA test because the genes are similar in origin, that is, they have a common ancestral origin in a particular area, a common ancestor.

"When I look at my own papers throughout the years," says Bonné-Tamir. "I find that I have been quite a pioneer in realizing the significance of combining the history of individuals or of populations with their biological attributes. This is now a leading undertaking in many studies which use, for example, mutations to estimate time to the most recent ancestors and alike."

What lines of inquiry are used in genetics? Dr. Charles R. Scriver wrote a chapter in Batsheva Bonné-Temir's book, titled *What are genes like that doing in a place like this? Human History and Molecular Prosopography*. The book title is: *Genetic Diversity Among Jews: Diseases and Markers at the DNA Level*. Bonné-Tamir, B. and Adam, A. Oxford University Press. 1992. With permission, an excerpt is reprinted below from page 319:

"When a disease clusters in a particular community, two lines of inquiry follow:
   1. Is the clustering caused by shared environmental exposure? Or is it explained by host susceptibility accountable to biological and/or cultural inheritance?
   2. If the explanation is biological, how are the determinants inherited? These lines of inquiry imply that a disease has two different histories, one biological, the other cultural. One involves genes (heredity), pathways of development

(ontogeny), and constitutional factors; the other, demography, migration and cultural practice. Neither history is mutually exclusive. Such thinking shifts the focus of inquiry from sick populations and incidence of disease to sick individuals and the cause of their particular disease. The person with the disease becomes the object of concern which is not the same as the disease the person has." (Page. 319).

After hearing from Dr. Scriver by email, I then emailed Stanley M. Diamond. He contacted writer, Barbara Khait, and got permission for me to reprint in this book some of what she wrote about Diamond's project. It's the chapter, "*Genetics Study Identifies At-risk relatives*" from *Celebrating the Family* published by Ancestry.com Publishing. Check out the Web site at: http://shops.ancestry.com/product.asp?productid=2625&shopid=128. Here's the reprinted article. Persons interested may go to the Web site for more information. I found out about Stanley M. Diamond from Dr. Scriver, since he mentioned Stanley M. Diamond's project in the book chapter Scriver wrote for Batsheva Bonné-Temir's book on *Genetic Diversity Among Jews: Diseases and Markers at the DNA Level*. Barbara Khait's chapter follows.

* * *

"In 1977, Stanley Diamond of Montreal learned he carried the beta-thalassemia genetic trait. Though common among people of Mediterranean, Middle Eastern, Southeast Asian and African descent, the trait is rare among descendants of eastern European Jews like Stan. His doctor made a full study of the family and identified Stanley's father as the source.

"Stan was spurred to action by a letter his brother received in 1991 from a previously unknown first cousin. Stan asked the cousin, "Do you carry the beta-thalassemia trait?" Though the answer was no, Stan began his journey to find out what other members of his family might be unsuspecting carriers.

"Later that year, Stan found a relative from his paternal grandmother's family, the Widelitz family. Again he asked, "Is there any incidence of anemia in your family?" His newfound cousin answered, "Oh, you mean beta-thalassemia? It's all over the family!"

"There was no question now that the trait could now be traced to Stan's grandmother, Masha Widelitz Diamond and that Masha's older brother Aaron also had to have been a carrier. Stan's next question: who passed the trait onto Masha and Aaron? Was it their mother, Sura Nowes, or their father, Jankiel Widelec?

"At the 1992 annual summer seminar on Jewish genealogy in New York City, Stan conferred with Or. Robert Desnick, who suggested that Stan's first step should be to determine whether the trait was related to a known mutation or a gene unique to his family. He advised Stan to seek out another Montrealer, Dr. Charles Scriver of McGill University-Montreal Children's Hospital. With the help of a grant, Dr. Scriver undertook the necessary DNA screening with the goal of determining the beta-thalassemia mutation.

"During this time, Stan began to research his family's history in earnest and identified their nineteenth century home town of Ostrow Mazowiecka in Poland. With the help of birth, marriage, and death records for the Jewish population of Ostrow Mazowiecka filmed by The Church of Jesus Christ of Latter-day Saints (LOS), Stan was able to construct his family tree.

"Late in 1993, Dr. Scriver faxed the news that the mutation had been identified and that it was, in fact, a novel mutation. Independently, Dr. Ariella Oppenheim at Jerusalem's Hebrew University-Hadassah Hospital mad e a similar discovery about a woman who had recently emigrated from the former Soviet Union.

""The likelihood that we were witnessing a DNA region 'identical by descent' in the two families was impressive. We had apparently discovered a familial relationship between Stanley and the woman in Jerusalem, previously unknown to either family," says Dr. Scriver.

"It wasn't very long ago when children born with thalassemia major seldom made it past the age of ten. Recent advances have increased life span but, to stay alive, these children must undergo blood transfusions every two to four weeks. And every night, they must receive painful transfusions of a special drug for up to twelve hours.

"The repeated blood transfusions lead to a buildup of iron in the body that can damage the heart, liver, and other organs. That's why, when the disease is misdiagnosed as mild chronic anemia, the prescription of additional iron is even more harmful. Right now, no cure exists for the disease, though medical experts say experimental bone-marrow transplants and gene-therapy procedures may one day lead to one.

"Stan's primary concern is that carriers of thalassemia trait may marry, often unaware that their mild chronic anemia may be something else. To aid in his search for carriers of his family's gene mutation of the beta-thalassemia trait, he founded and coordinates an initiative known as Jewish Records Indexing-Poland, an award-winning Internet-based index of Jewish vital records in Poland, with more than one million references. This database is helping Jewish families, particularly those at increased risk for hereditary conditions and diseases, trace their medical histories, as well as geneticists.

"Says Dr. Robert Burk, professor of epidemiology at the Albert Einstein College of Medicine at Yeshiva University, and principal investigator for the Cancer Longevity, Ancestry and Lifestyle (CLAL) study in the Jewish population (currently focusing on prostate cancer), "Through the establishment of a searchable database from Poland, careful analysis of the relationship between individuals will be possible at both the familial and the molecular level.

"This will afford us the opportunity to learn not only more about the Creator's great work, but will also allow (us) researchers new opportunities to dissect the cause of many diseases in large established pedigrees."

Several other medical institutions, including Yale University's Cancer Genetics Program, the Epidemiology-Genetics Program at the Johns Hopkins School of Medicine, and Mount Sinai Hospital's School of Medicine have recognized Diamond's work as an outstanding application of knowing one's family history and as a guide to others who may be trying to trace their medical histories, particularly those at increased risk for hereditary conditions and diseases.

In February 1998, in a breakthrough effort, Stanley discovered another member of his family who carried the trait. He found the descendants of Jankiel's niece and nephew—first cousins who married—David Lustig and his wife, Fanny Bengelsdorf. This was no ordinary find—he located the graves by using a map of the Ostrow Mazowiecka section of Chicago's Waldheim Cemetery and contacted the person listed as the one paying for perpetual care, David and Fanny's grandson, Alex.

"It turned out Alex, too, had been diagnosed as a beta-thalassemia carrier by his personal physician fifteen years earlier. The discovery that David and Fanny's descendants were carriers of the beta-thalassemia trait convinced Stan, Dr. Scriver, and Dr. Oppenheim that Hersz Widelec, born in 1785, must be the source of the family's novel mutation.

"'This groundbreaking work helps geneticists all over the world understand the trait and its effects on one family,' says Dr. Oppenheim. "A most important contribution of Stanley Diamond's work is increasing the awareness among his relatives and others to the possibility that they carry a genetic trait which with proper measures, can be prevented in future generations. In addition. the work has demonstrated the power of modern genetics in identifying distant relatives, and helps to clarify how genetic diseases are being spread throughout the world."

For more information about thalassemia, contact Cooley's Anemia Foundation (129-09 26th Avenue. Flushing, New York, 11354; by phone 800-522-7222; or online at www.cooleysanemia.org). For more about Stanley Diamond's research. visit his Web site (www.diamondgen.org).

Thalassemia is not only carried by people living today in Mediterranean lands. The first Polish (not Jewish) carrier of Beta-Thal was discovered in the last few years in Bialystok, Poland. Stanley Diamond met with the Director of the Hematology Institute in Warsaw in November 2002, and the Director of the Hematology Institute in Warsaw indicated that they now have identified 52 carriers. Check out these Web sites listed below if the subject intrigues you.

"Genealogy with an extra reason"…Beta-Thalassemia Research Projec
www.diamondgen.org

JTA genetic disorder and Polish Jewish history
www.jta.org/page_view_story.asp?intarticleid=11608&intcategoryid=5

IAJGS Lifetime Achievement Award
www.jewishgen.org/ajgs/awards.html

Jewish Records Indexing—Poland
www.jri-poland.org

*   *   *

Molecular Revolution

Geneticists today are making inroads in new areas such as phenomics and ancestral genetics. Batsheva Bonné-Tamir, PhD, http://www.tau.ac.il/medicine/USR/bonnétamirb.htm or http://www.tau.ac.il/medicine/ at Tel-Aviv University, Israel, is Head of the National Laboratory for the Genetics of Israeli Populations (with Mia Horowitz) and Director of the Shalom and Varda Yoran Institute for Genome Research Tel-Aviv. She is also on the faculty of the Department of Human Genetics and Molecular Medicine, Sackler School of Medicine,

Dr. Bonné-Tamir states that "One of *my* most impressive conclusions from the advancement in the last few years and the accumulation of knowledge in the fields of genetics and medicine, is the *molecular* revolution based on immense sophistication of lab techniques. This is really responsible for the recent increased emphasis on the *human-social-anthropological* aspects that affect biological diversity."

Bonné-Tamir explains, "At a meeting in 1973, in my paper on **Merits and Difficulties in Studies of Middle Eastern Isolates**, I said that 'The Middle Eastern isolates have emphasized again the fertile and necessary interrelationship between history and genetics.'"

Do historical events influence genes? "Comparative studies in population genetics are often undertaken in order to attempt reconstruction of historical and migratory movements based on gene frequencies," says Bonné-Tamir. "The Samaritans and Karaites offer opportunities in the opposite direction, for example, to learn the influence of historical events on gene frequencies."

In another paper in 1979 on **Analysis of Genetic Data on Jewish Populations,** Dr. Bonné-Temir wrote that "Our purpose in studying the differences and similarities between various Jewish populations was not to determine whether a Jewish race exists. Nor was it to discover the original genes of 'ancient Hebrews,' or to retrieve genetic characteristics in the historical development of the Jews.

"Rather, it was to evaluate the extent of 'heterogeneity' in the separate populations, to construct a profile of each population as shaped by the genetic data, and to draw inferences about the possible influences of dispersion, migration, and admixture processes on the genetic composition of these populations."

In 1999, Dr. Bonné-Temir organized an international symposium on *Genomic Views of Jewish History*. "And unfortunately, the many papers presented were never published," says Bonné-Temir.

Molecular Genealogy Research Projects

Genomic views of any ethnic group's history are important for further study. Whether you are taking the skeptic's position or the genomic view of your cultural history, biology does have a cultural component that needs to be analyzed scientifically. Finding flaws or benefits in research studies of any kind is the way to find inroads to truths. How else can facts change and knowledge progress?

Molecular genealogy has joined efforts with molecular genetics. How can this information help you in family history research? Ugo A. Perego, MS. Senior Project Administrator, Molecular Genealogy Research Project, Brigham Young University, http://molecular-genealogy.byu.edu, says, "I believe that DNA is the next thing in genealogy—the tool for the 21st century family historians. In the past 20 years, the genealogical world has been revolutionized by the introduction of the Internet.

"An increasing number of people are becoming interested in searching for their ancestors because through emails and websites a large world of family history information is now available to them. The greatest contribution of molecular methods to family history is the fact that in some instances family relationships and blocked genealogies can be extended even in the absence of written records.

"Adoptions, illegitimacies, names that have been changes, migrations, wars, fire, flood, etc. are all situations in which a record may become unavailable. However, no one can change our genetic composition, which we have received by those that came before us.

"Currently, DNA testing is an effective approach to help with strict paternal and maternal lines thanks to the analysis and comparison of the Y chromosome (male line) and mitochondrial DNA (female line) in individuals that have reason to believe the existence of a common paternal or maternal ancestor.

"A large database of genetic and genealogical data is currently been built by the BYU Center for Molecular Genealogy and the Sorenson Molecular Genealogy Foundation. This database will contain thousands of pedigree charts and DNA from people from all over the world. Currently it has already over 35,000 participants in it.

"The purpose of this database is to provide additional knowledge in reconstructing family lines other than the paternal and maternal, by using a large number of autosomal DNA (the DNA found in the non-sex chromosomes). This research, known as the Molecular Genealogy Research Project is destined to take DNA for genealogists to the next level."

For additional reading, please visit the BYU's Molecular Genealogy Research Project's two Web sites. Another good source of information is at www.relativegenetics.com, a company specialized in Y chromosome analysis for family studies.

What Are Your Genes Doing In That Temporary Container?

Have you ever wondered what your genes are doing in your "temporary container" before they move on and change and where they have traveled during the past 40,000 years or more? When you have your DNA tested, work with the lab and DNA testing company, and ask them to explain to you how the 25 Y-chromosome markers you had tested as a male or mtDNA as a female help you determine your ancestry or find any matches similar to your DNA in a database. Read the frequently asked questions files of DNA testing companies online. Ask questions by email.

Sons inherit their mtDNA from their own mothers. Then mothers pass mtDNA on to their daughters. Sons also inherit the Y-chromosome from their fathers, but do not pass it to their daughters. Women don't have Y chromosomes.

The mtDNA is passed down from mother to son and mother to daughter through the cytoplasm (the cell contents surrounding the nucleus) in the egg. Only the daughters pass on their mtDNA to their daughters. And sons pass their Y-chromosomes to their sons, but those sons carry the mtDNA of their own mothers.

Even though both sons and daughters are formed from the union of a sperm and an egg, only the daughters will pass their mtDNA (which is the same as their great grandmother's on their maternal side and still further back to the first founder of their mtDNA group. Only daughters will pass the mtDNA on to the next generation.

Each lab has different methods of reporting their results, but you can use DNA test results as a tool for learning family history. Join DNA mailing lists and research or ask questions of the DNA testing firms specializing in genealogy by genetics about how many mutations occur in how many generations.

Here's how you can do your own research independently of any laboratory that tested your own DNA if you're curious about Y-chromosome DNA tests. Males take Y-chromosome DNA tests to find out paternal ancestry lineages. Males also can have their mtDNA checked, but women don't have a Y chromosome. So women only can check their maternal lineages with mitochondrial (mtDNA) tests. According to Alastair Greenshields who runs Ybase at http://www.ybase.org, "Ybase is a free and open database which allows people to enter their Y-chromosome haplotype details independently of the laboratory they were tested at. Anyone can contribute to it and anyone can explore it."

The database can accept results for any of the 36 Y-chromosome markers currently in use along with other genealogical information. "Ybase is searchable for exact haplotype matches and/or near misses," says Greenshields. "Surnames, variant spellings and other relevant names can also be searched for, which is especially useful for the genealogist wishing to locate and contact others that share their surname and have had their DNA tested."

Most researchers that recognize their Y-chromosome cannot identify an actual individual and are happy to share their results online in an effort to find their DNA cousins and genetic roots. "Genealogical research coupled with DNA testing is already proving a very powerful method of substantiating ancestry," Greenshields explains. "And Ybase is sure to grow in line with this upward trend, benefiting the genealogical community as a whole."

Are male and female genetic lineages studied for different purposes? "Ybase is solely intended for Y-DNA and not mtDNA. A database of the latter would be so general and broad, given the nature of how mtDNA is passed on, as to be of little value to a researcher," Greenshields says.

Below are a couple of explanations on Y-DNA Alastair Greenshields wrote for two different people with entirely different backgrounds who needed the whole thing explained to them. "They explain essentially the same terms but have been 'dumbed down' to varying extents. Please feel entirely free to copy them verbatim or adjust as you deem necessary," says Greenshields.

To answer my question to Greenshields on how to interpret the results of DNA tests for Y-chromosome analysis for ancestry, he's explained it well in terms that most people can understand.

"Imagine a very long rope, some of which is lying across your desk. This is the DNA strand," Greenshields says. "It just happens to be the length of rope called 'Your Y-chromosome'.

"Now look at the bit that lies across your desk and grasp the rope with both hands, about half a meter apart. This is a 'marker' or 'locus' (Latin for 'place'). We'll call it DYS19.

"In between your hands, imagine that bit of rope is divided into 14 equally-spaced segments. If you look very closely at the segments, you can see that each one has a bit of writing on it, which reads TAGA.

"This is simply the DNA code for each repeat. Therefore the marker DYS19=14 repeats. Or if I ask you, 'What allele have you got for DYS19?' You can tell me '14'. (Allele effectively means the number of repeats.) For example, DYS19 has about nine possibilities (between 11 and 19).

"If you do the same at lots of different markers or loci (plural of locus), you'll get a whole series of numbers (DYS19=14, DYS388=15, DYS461=11 etc.). This is your 'haplotype'. It doesn't matter whether it is 20 or 200 numbers in length. This series of numbers is still called your haplotype.

"Now you are going to make some rope for your new son. You are pretty good at making rope and usually you can copy your own precisely, but this time you made it slightly too short. There are now 13 repeats. (Technically this is called a 'mutation' which can occur when an enzyme mis-types the DNA code). It still works perfectly well so your son keeps it and is very happy! There, you have it—DNA in a nutshell! (Be aware that your repeats, like the stock-market, may go up as well as down, but for entirely different reasons.)

Genealogy and the Y Chromosome

"DNA for the use of genealogy usually requires an analysis of your Y-chromosome," Greenshields explains. "Only males have this particular chromosome and the DNA code held within it is passed down from father to son (virtually) unchanged. Provided there is an unbroken paternal line between two males, that is both share a g-g-g-g-g-grandfather, their Y-chromosome DNA will be the same."

When the DNA is analyzed, many small sections are looked at. Presently, the testing companies look for anywhere between 10 and 26 sections or 'markers.' "At any one of the markers, the code will repeat itself, for example, 15 times," Greenshields explains. "If the marker is called DYS19, we can give the result DYS19=15."

If you analyze several of these markers, you end up with a 'haplotype'.

Thus you can compare haplotypes to see if you are related. "I say 'virtually' unchanged, as the DNA can change slightly over time due to 'mutations'—small errors formed when the DNA is copied," says Greenshields. "When comparing the haplotypes from two people, this will show up as a 'mismatch'—where, for example, DYS 19=14."

These mutations are useful by themselves and occur at a fairly steady rate over time. "It also gives us the great variability that we observe over populations," says Greenshields. "If the mutations did not occur, every male would have identical Y-chromosomes. Also, within DNA/genealogy studies, if many mismatches occur when comparing two male haplotypes, we can say that they are not related."

So you can see, DNA can be a very useful tool when comparing 'suspected' relatives. "But there is one caveat, however," Greenshields emphasizes. "You must share a surname, or have a very good reason to believe you are related. DNA alone will not identify your relatives from any other random person."

For example, you will probably share the same haplotype to at least someone in your home-town, but having a similar or same surname will raise the probabilities significantly. "DNA is a tool that should be overlaid on the existing genealogical records," notes Greenshield. "It can be an excellent way of deciding on further avenues of research, or indeed defining that there are several distinct lines within your family name."

Understanding HLA Genes (White Blood Cells)

HLA genes are white blood cells. Anthropologists look at white blood cells called by the scientific name of HLA genes to study genetic drift. If you have a research need to learn about tissue typing, you might want to read about understanding the HLA genes. Tissue typing is usually done on white blood cells, or leukocytes. The markers are referred to as human leukocyte antigens (HLA). A good starting point is to read the definitions and excerpts about tissue typing testing on the *'About' Health and Fitness* Web site at:
http://thyroid.about.com/library/immune/blimm25.htm?terms=Human+Leukocyte+Antigen.

"My personal view of the HLA genes and genetic genealogy is that the two will almost certainly not be mixed in the near future on a commercial basis," says Greenshield. "My reasoning is two-fold. First, the L in HLA stands for leukocyte/leucocyte (Gk leuko=white). The test involves looking at 'white' blood cells." This would involve taking a blood sample (or possibly sampling a site of infection) and a trained phlebotomist being on hand. The Brigham Young University (BYU) study *used to* have participants give blood (of which HLA typing is possibly involved)."

Ugo A. Perego, MS, Senior Project Administrator, Molecular Genealogy Research Project, BYU emphasizes, "*We stopped using blood last summer.* All our collections are now based on a simple 45 seconds rinse *using mouthwash.*"

"Your average genealogists are only willing to swab the inside of their mouths," says Greenshields. "Even a pin prick of blood would, possibly, be too much to ask of one's suspected relatives." DNA testing for ancestry only requires a swab of felt or cotton on the inner cheek or rinsing your mouth with mouthwash.

"Secondly, the HLA system can provide information or guides to genetic disposition to disease. Given the apprehension about giving a cheek swab to be 'junk-DNA tested' for the Y-chromosome, having HLA alleles typed, compared, and possibly posted to the net would discourage all but the hardy," says Greenshields. "I believe HLA testing for genealogical studies will remain under the domain of research into genetic drift and anthropological studies."

If you ever need a tissue donor or have to get your tissue typed for medical reasons, that's when the HLA genes play a major role in tissue typing. Interestingly, when small communities are isolated for long periods of time, and bottlenecks pare down the population to only a few founders, genetic drift may occur. That's when the anthropologists and evolutionary biologists look at the HLA genes.

With some DNA testing companies offering racial percentages tests, Y-chromosome tests, and mtDNA tests, what is being done with mtDNA testing for maternal lineages? How can we trace female relatives or ancestors who leave no written records of their name or existence?

Will studies of HLA genes be used by others in various fields as research now is used by anthropologists studying genetic drift, scientists studying tissue differentiation, or physicians looking at how white cells fight infection?

Dr. Peter Reed has a PhD in Human Genetics from the University of Oxford and was a pioneer in the use of STR genetic markers in medical research. He explains here that HLA genes primarily determine how our blood cells recognize and react to other cells present in our bodies. In particular, this makes HLA genes important in how our body responds to 'foreign bodies.'

For example, the HLA genes as white blood cells, fight infection. When bacteria or viruses enter our bodies, the HLA genes are there to do battle. When organs or tissue are transplanted, HLA genes have to be considered.

They would attack the foreign tissue placed in the body. "When people talk about blood typing or tissue matching, on the whole, they are referring to determining some aspect of the set of HLA genes," says Reed. "HLA genes are perhaps the most variable of all human genes. Across the population, some HLA genes have dozens of different forms of genes or 'alleles.'"

The result is that two randomly chosen people are unlikely to share identical HLA genes. "Even within families, there is a good chance that each family member has a different set of HLA genes," says Reed. "That's why finding a 'suitable match' for a transplant can be difficult." It's also the reason why we all react differently to infections. On the plus side, HLA genes (white blood cells) can deal with all the different infections we get during our lives, usually without being aware of them.

Apart from the obvious medical importance of a role in responding to infection and transplantation, there is another role. It's perhaps one of the primary reasons that HLA genes are some of the most intensely studied of all human genes.

"This relates to the role HLA genes play in determining how our blood cells respond to the other cells of the body," says Reed. "In certain circumstances, some of a person's own cells are mistaken as 'foreign bodies.' These cells are responded to as if they were an infection." The technical jargon for this is called auto-immunity.

"This can result in disease. This sort of problem is believed to be one of the underlying causes many fairly common diseases, more appropriately termed 'conditions'. Such conditions include Rheumatoid Arthritis and Juvenile Diabetes," says Reed. "A connection between particular types of HLA genes and certain conditions was first recognized over thirty years ago." Since then many connections between HLA and human conditions have been identified.

These genes are obviously very important in human health, and are often suspected as being the major genetic causes of numerous conditions. Consequently, there are a number of clinical programs where HLA genes are screened (particularly in children) to research and even determine the risk of later disease.

"One aspect of the high variability of HLA genes, is that certain types (alleles) of certain HLA genes have been found to be geographically/ethnically distributed," says Reed. "For example, some alleles of some HLA genes may be more frequent in Japan than in England. Therefore there is some possible utility in the use of HLA genes in determining ancestry from different geographical locations. However, because the HLA genes are only a small fraction of all our genes, examining HLA genes alone is not likely to be very informative."

"Because HLA genes, like almost all our other genes, are shuffled and mixed as they are passed on from parents to children, it's difficult to determine the exact set of HLA genes of even one or two generations previous," Reed says. "So they have little utility in determining recent ancestry." There could be some utility of HLA for genealogy. "This could be so in certain circumstances," Reed explains, "but the hurdles mentioned above will need to be overcome. I'm exploring this further."

According to Ann Turner, Genealogy-DNA List Administrator, at: http://lists.rootsweb.com/index/other/Miscellaneous/GENEALOGY-DNA.html, an excellent Web site for explaining HLA is located at the Web site: http://www.med.umich.edu/trans/public/hla/hla_&_you.html.

"This HLA Web site diagrams the inheritance patterns. It says HLA is on gene 6, but it means chromosome 6," reports Turner. "You also can learn about linkage disequilibrium at this site. Some genes in the HLA system are close to one another. That makes the alleles, which are a form of a gene, also linked together closely and inherited as one unit, or haplotype." That's the original context for the word 'haplotype.' Also look at: http://www.hokkaido.bc.jrc.or.jp/laboratory/laboratory500_eng.htm, Turner notes.

Understanding Your Maternal Lineages—mtDNA

MtDNA shows ancestry passed from mother to daughter from a single common ancestor or founder. Every human owes his or her ancestry to the ultimate "Mitochondrial Eve" the first woman to walk out of Africa and head towards Yemen around 154,000 years ago, give or take a few thousand years.

If we study mitochondrial "Eve" then we have to study Y-chromosome "Adam." We have to ask whether mtDNA diversity is higher than Y-chromosome diversity because mtDNA developed and mutated at a different rate than Y chromosomes if we look to prehistoric ancestry lines.

Usually, studies of mtDNA show either women had a more diverse genetic history or some communities were founded by very few female founders. For example, H haplogroup of mtDNA found in a large percentage of Europeans may have begun in the Dordogne valley of what is now France and/or in northern Spain about 21,000 years ago, but before that, H haplogroup may have had an ancestor somewhere else.

That common ancestor was one woman who had at least two daughters who survived to have more daughters and who lived somewhere in the Middle East. At some point back in time, H haplogroup arose from a still more ancient common ancestor, another woman, who lived outside of Europe.

What we see now are the mutations that occurred over thousands of years since haplogroup H mtDNA reached Europe and expanded to cover today all of Europe from Iceland to the Urals. H haplogroup mtDNA today is found in places as far apart as Bashkortostan in the Urals and Iceland, Scotland, Spain, Norway, Austria, Turkey, Crete, Ukraine, Italy, and Bulgaria.

MtDNA haplogroups are classified as A, B, C, D, E, F, G H through J, K, M, N, O, P, R, and T through Z. Then some are given little sub classifications such as U1, U2, U3, U4, U5, U6, U7, and various types of U found in mostly in India. New mtDNA haplogroups are still be uncovered. M is a super haplogroup divided into various groups of M such as M1 and M11. As ancient burials are uncovered, different mtDNA haplogroups turn up that are not here today because they are very ancient and did not survive because some women had only sons and some daughters didn't survive to reproduce.

Using Your Own DNA Test Results as a Genealogy Tool

It's good to have a mentor to answer questions about your test results until you are able to do your own research on the Web. If you're a lay person, where can you learn enough molecular genetics to get a handle on DNA test results and untangle ancestral roots? If you've ever wondered why *your* genes are not where you thought they were supposed to be (in geographic location on a map), that topic of research is called molecular prosopography. See the Web site: www.linacre.ox.ac.uk/research/prosop/prosopo.stm.

Prosopography is an independent science of social history embracing genealogy, onomastics and demography. Prosopography is all about human history and genes that travel because your genes have both a cultural and a biological component. The cultural component includes onomastics which is the study of the origin of a name and its geographical and historical utilization. Onomastics includes the study of how and when place-names were originated and used. Then there's toponymics. Toponymics is the study of names related to a place or region. See http://libraryweb.utep.edu/onomastics.html or http://www.kami.demon.co.uk/gesithas/biblio/bib08.html. And you probably know demography, is the interdisciplinary study of human populations. Demography deals with social characteristics of the population and their development. So you'd find more information on demography by researching population studies. Phenomics is the science of customizing, tailoring, and individualizing medicines and other health treatments to the total human genome of one person.

The age of one medicine or hormone fits all is gone. As a tool, phenomics also can be applied to herbal remedies, food supplements, vitamins and minerals, hormones, and other formulas adjusted to an individual's total genome. If you have a genetic risk for a certain disease, perhaps you can find out what way there is to prevent it by using phenomics as a tool for customizing your treatment or working on prevention strategies of lifestyle, diet, or medicine.

Family history DNA testing is a new way to approach biological research. Genealogy and genetics are forms of hunting and gathering that persist. First you start with transcribed oral history. We are foragers in molecular family history.

Molecular genealogy uses DNA testing (human genetics) as a tool for untangling ancestral and recent family roots. Here's an introduction to family DNA testing to be used with oral history gathering and genealogy.

Start your family history time capsule, gift basket, scrapbook, genetic genealogy, or begin a small business publicizing DNA testing for genealogy. The place for genetic genealogy is in an archives, library, museum, or good storage place.

Future generations need a DNA history of as many ancestors as they can find willing to participate and to create oral histories. Genetics is the most mathematical/statistical of the biological sciences. We have fields such as bioinformatics that combine computers and biological information. Family historians need a bridge to fill the gap between such a mathematical science as genetics and genealogy, often based on records and oral histories.

The oral history would be transcribed on acid-free paper in hard, bound copy. Photos and other memorabilia could be added. Then the basic archive would be copied onto disks such as a CD, DVD, or other, stored in a computer and on video and audio tape.

Another copy would be saved as a multimedia presentation with text, sound, voice, photos, illustrations, and video/audio and saved on a disk to be played on screen with a home entertainment player or in a computer. You could put a smaller file online on a Web site. This molecular biography would represent not only the life of a person, but a history of the person's DNA test results, racial percentages, ethnicity, if known, and anything else about the DNA sequence as far as geographic location or even medical history, if desired, in a more private file for relatives. This is where genetics joins with genealogy.

We not only have a family history to archive, but now a genome, or at least a record of the matrilineal and patrilineal ancestry by DNA. We have the markers and the sequences. The idea is to learn enough about DNA testing and genealogy to understand what those sequences and markers mean.

What can we learn about ancestry through the mitochondrial DNA (for women and men) the Y chromosome only for men, and other markers on the genome? What should we look at to view the percentages of races such as Native American, African, East Asian, or Indo-European (Europe, Middle East, and India)?

What do these sequences tell us about our ancestry? If there's no such thing as race, what geographic locations of our ancestors are we viewing back in time when we look at the genetic markers?

What dates are we looking at—a few generations ago or 21,000 years? What do our transitions and mutations mean over a long span of time? What foods, medicines, therapies, and climates are best for our customized, individual molecular profiles?

How do we read and interpret those genetic markers? Where does genealogy and oral history fit in? Family history—genealogy—now has joined up with molecular genetics and evolutionary anthropology. And included with genealogy is the tradition of transcribing and recording oral history, diary journaling and restoration, time capsules, biography, scrap booking, videography, and photography.

The genome has reached the genealogist. Family history today is multimedia and molecular, historical and futuristic.

"Progress in our knowledge of the genome and of its function has been extremely rapid since the development, in the mid-eighties, of the Polymerase Chain Reaction," says Professor of Genetics, Guido Barbujani, (Department of Biology, University of Ferrara, Italy.) Dipartimento di Biologia, Universita' di Ferrara via L. Borsari 46, I-44100 Ferrara, Italia. See his Web site at: http://www.unife.it/genetica/Guido/Guido.html.

Dr. Barbujani's fields of interest include human population and molecular genetics and evolution, and I've read many of his articles in the various journals of genetics and research books, such as *Archaeogenetics*: DNA and the population prehistory of Europe published by the McDonald Institute Monographs.

"By that method, minimal quantities of DNA can be studied, which has opened the field for a number of previously hard-to-imagine applications, ranging from gene therapy to the prediction of interactions among genes, from the sequencing of entire genomes to the retrieval of DNA sequences from extinct organisms," Barbujani explains.

"DNA technologies proved so powerful that people tend to forget about their limitations. Still, limitations exist, especially in the field of genealogical reconstructions, and future technical advancements are unlikely to be of great help.

"Consider this: Each of us has two parents, four grandparents, eight grand-grandparents, and so on. In principle, only ten generations ago (around 1750 AD) we had 1024 different ancestors. In fact, chances are our ancestors were less than 1024, because consanguineous marriages likely occurred at various stages. But even if we had only 200 independent ancestors ten generations ago, each of them contributed to our 30,000 or so genes.

"On the other hand, only one of them transmitted to us her mitochondrial DNA and, if we are males, from only one of them did we inherit our Y chromosome," Barbujani reveals. "The other 198 or 199 ancestors' contributions to our genotype are of course equally important, but there is no easy way to figure them out."

"Indeed, at every generation recombination created new associations of genes along our chromosomes, except for the mitochondrial DNA and for part of the Y chromosome, which do not recombine.

In this way, traits of DNA coming from different ancestors have been assembled in a mosaic that cannot be disentangled a posteriori, in which each piece has a different, and possibly very different, origin. In short, it is an illusion to think that our mitochondrial DNA (or our Y chromosome) may allow us to understand our family history.

"These are small parts of our genome, and hence contain information on but a small bit of our biological history," says Barbujani. "Other ancestors have transmitted to us many more genes than the ancestors from whom we inherited our mitochondrial DNA, and they may have come from different parts of the world."

"That may sound frustrating to some, but population genetics has something important to tell us in this regard. Population histories are much easier to reconstruct than individual histories, because chance phenomena have a much greater impact on the latter.

"When a large number of individuals are jointly analyzed, rather robust evolutionary inferences may be drawn, even if some members of the sample have had an unusual family history. By combining measures of genetic diversity, among populations and among individuals, with the evidence coming from mitochondrial and Y-chromosome genealogies, population geneticists have shown very clearly that each population contains a large proportion of all humankind's alleles, around 85 percent, on average.

"This finding has several implications. One is: should most humans disappear because of some global catastrophe, and should only one community survive, the loss of genetic diversity would be very limited, around 15 percent. That might or might not be reassuring, but is true.

"Secondly, although many tend to think that humans come in clear racial clusters, that is not true; if, on average, populations contain 85 percent of the global human diversity, two individuals from very distant localities can be just 15 percent more different genetically than members of the same population (unless the latter are relatives, of course). Third, if genetic diversity is so high among members of the same population, the only possible explanation is that those populations incorporated, through time, contributions from other populations at a rather high rate.

"In other words, our ancestors spent most of their evolutionary time in communities connected by extensive migratory exchanges, and not in isolated groups. Through migration, alleles of African, Asian and European origin ended up all over the world, and no biologically recognizable race evolved in our species. Therefore, it is impossible to define our origin by studying our DNA, but if it were possible, we would probably find that our roots are spread over much of the world.

"As Jonathan Marks remarked, today convincing people that there is no such thing as a human race is probably as difficult as, in the 17th century, to convince people that the earth rotates around the sun and not vice versa. However, this is a scientific fact, and perhaps the single most significant result of human evolutionary studies. Everybody can tell a Nigerian from a Japanese person, but if we move from Nigeria to Japan we shall never find a sharp boundary separating two well-distinct groups.

"Rather, we shall notice that the genetic features of people change continuously, in a gradient, and that each community harbors substantial biological differences among its members. The best way to summarize these concepts, I think, is by a slogan invented by the French anthropologist André Langaney: *Tous parents, tous différénts*. We are all relatives, and we are all different."

Here are some definitions you might want to peruse before we go into the next chapter on personalizing family history records with the results of DNA tests. If you are a historian or genealogist, it would be useful to be able to discuss possible DNA testing with your clients. Molecular tools to family history research open doors to new subjects.

Useful DNA Definitions for Historians and Genealogists Interested in Molecular Anthropology/Archaeology

* **Genome.** A person's genome is one set of his (or her) | genes. The human genes, which control a cell's structure, | operation, and division, are located in the cell's nucleus. The | full human genome (estimated at 50,000 to 100,000 genes) is present in every cell-nucleus, even though many genes are| inactive in cells which have some specialized functions (the| "differentiated" cells).

* **Genes and Chromosomes.** Genes are composed of segments of DNA. In normal cell-nuclei, the DNA is distributed among 46 chromosomes (23 inherited at conception from a person's father, and 23 from the mother). Each chromosome consists of one very long strand of DNA and numerous proteins, which are required for successful management of the long DNA molecule. The longest chromosomes each "carry" thousands of genes. Every time a cell divides, the cell must duplicate the 46 chromosomes and must distribute one copy of each to the two resulting cells.

* **The Code.** The DNA of each chromosome is composed of units—nucleotides" of four different types (A, T, G, C). These nucleotides are linked to each other in linear fashion. The sequence of the four types of nucleotides is critical, because the sequence produces the "code" which (a) determines the function of each particular gene, (b) identifies the gene's start-point and stop-point along the DNA strand, and (c) permits certain regulatory functions. The code of the human genome consists of more than a billion nucleotides.

* **The Mitochondrial DNA (mtDNA).** Outside the nucleus, human cells also have some "foreign" DNA located in structures called the mitochondria. This small and separate set of DNA does not participate in the 46 human chromosomes, and is not part of "the genomic DNA." The mitochondria are inherited from the mother.

These genetic term definitions are from the book titled: *Confirmation that Ionizing Radiation Can Induce Genomic Instability: What is Genomic Instability, and Why Is It So Important?* John W. Gofman, M.D., Ph.D., and Egan O'Connor, Executive Director, CNR. Spring, 1998. The excerpt of definitions from Dr. Gofman's essays, such as what is quoted above is reprinted with permission. See excerpts from the book at the Web site at:
http://www.ratical.org/radiation/CNR/GenomicInst.html.
All the definitions from Dr. Gofman's essays are available for reproduction in other publications. Please do cite the title and above URL so people who wish to study the complete work can do so. For more information see the Web site at: CNR page (http://www.ratical.org/radiation/CNR/). For further information, contact the publisher, David Ratcliffe, "rat haus reality press" at:
http://www.ratical.org/rhrPress.html.

CHAPTER TWO

Personalizing Family History Records with DNA Testing

Diaries and DNA testing personalize family history records. DNA family databases and scrap booking are more valuable when linked together. It's time to compile a written and illustrated family tree time capsule in any or all of various media—print, pictures, video, audio, for the Web, in a scrapbook form of stories, anecdotes, experiences, photos, journal writings, and memorabilia that also includes DNA testing.

DNA test results and autobiographies also may highlight the important events that you want remembered. In the future, families may be able to archive the sequences of their entire genome—all their genes—into a database to be kept along with photos, video, audio, crafts, and memorabilia marking the life experiences, events, rites of passage, and highlights focused around a central issue.

You can piece together records of women's clubs, diaries, and DNA tests and look at your maternal lineages. String together military pension or service records, village societies, or Census records and city directories, and link your paternal lineage from voter lists and court records to Y-chromosome test results.

The file or database could be passed onto other family members and the genome given to health care professionals to customize therapy or treatment, tailor foods and vitamins or supplements, or create a living video biography. For now, whole genome DNA testing is expensive, and what are affordable include the matrilineal and patrilineal lineages and the percentages of races.

For family historians, there are also the surname databases and message boards on the Web. And for tracing female ancestors, there are marriage certificates, birth records, court records, church and synagogue records, records of teachers, factory workers, census records, social and immigrant records, women's publications, clubs, insurance records, deeds and wills, and other records that reveal more than the words, "and wife."

The 1850 US Census was the first census to name all members of a household, their birthplaces, and whether married within the year. By 1870, the US Census asked whether one's parents were foreign born. And a decade later, the 1880 US Census named relationships to the head of household.

By 1900, the US Census included the number of years married, number of children born and who of the children were living. They also added immigration and naturalization data. Native Americans had special censuses. So you can also look at school censuses and state and local censuses as well as city directories published until 1976. Years ago when people had no phones, the city directory was one way to locate families.

In creating a "family history memorabilia time capsule" or database that includes DNA testing, you can include small crafts such as braided hair embroidery as art, craft, needlework, preserved clothing or wedding gowns restored and wrapped. You'd index where the craft work or clothing is located, and the index or list of memorabilia would go into your scrapbook, database, or time capsule. What new item that you might add, would be the family's DNA, the male and female mtDNA and the male Y chromosome, plus a racial percentages DNA test.

Records may be copies and stored in many ways—as Web sites, printed books, diaries, on CDs and DVDs, as video and audio tapes, as oral history transcripts printed out in text, or as a photo scrapbook with captions. Or you can create a multimedia presentation combining text, voice, video, photographs, music, and commentary.

You would ask as many relatives as you can find to lightly rub a felt tip or pad, cytobrush, or a swish of mouthwash in their mouths and send the samples packaged and labeled separately to a DNA for genealogy testing company. With all those entries in your time capsule, your descendants (or your clients' if you do family history research) will have a better idea of who any particular family was as people (rather than some anonymous photos).

You can even search antique stores and flea markets and the people listed on the Web. Some genealogists rescue old photos and are listed on the Web. Check to see whether any photos found in certain locations might be your family members or those of your clients if you are a genealogist or family history researcher.

So you wipe a felt swab or small brush across the inside of your cheek and mail it to a DNA testing company. Or you swish a type of mouth wash and expectorate it into a container and mail it back to a DNA testing company emphasizing testing and/or researching genealogy by DNA analysis. Some of these companies may also have a division that tests DNA for forensic purposes, and other firms may give the DNA to a laboratory for actual testing and then send you the results with information on how to further research your ancient lineages or genealogy for more recent DNA matches.

What comes back to you in the mail a few weeks later are a print out, perhaps a CD, or a mailing on paper and/or email table of some of your DNA sequences. Now it's your job to find out what the sequences mean. Most companies have frequently answered questions message boards and some firms will email you answers to your questions. Other companies may offer to store your DNA or a certain length of time. So check with the company on what it offers regarding DNA testing and genealogy questions answered.

"The state of identity testing is such that people should have a specific hypothesis that they want to test," says Harry Ostrer, M.D,

Professor of Pediatrics, Pathology, and Medicine Director, Human Genetics Program New York University School of Medicine.

"Do Susan Smith and I share a common matrilineal ancestor? Do Jeffrey Jones and I (if male) share a common patrilineal ancestor?" Dr. Ostrer asks. "Hoping to discover something unanticipated is unrealistic. It is very unlikely that amateur genealogists will discover that they had Amerindian ancestry unless they had a strong reason to expect so.

"The problem of course is that many people are searching for roots and hoping that genetic testing will fill the gap for absence of familial oral histories," Dr. Ostrer explains. "Unfortunately, there are no shortcuts to the work of the genealogist. With the Internet, email and a heightened awareness of genealogy, the tools—word-of-mouth and access to vital records—are more accessible."

According to Dr. Harry Ostrer's article, "A Genetic Profile of Contemporary Jewish Populations," in *Nature Reviews/Genetics*, Vol. 2, November 2001 (Science and Society), p. 895, Macmillan Magazines Ltd, "The Ashkenazi Jewish population in Eastern Europe expanded rapidly, growing from an estimated 10,000-15,000 people in 1500 to 2 million in 1800 and 8 million in 1939 (REF.34)."

Compare that profile to the group of people you're researching. What's the individual's genetic profile? How does it compare to the oral history profile or the written record profile, either social or medical, ethnic, or industrial?

Consider the group of people you may belong to on one or both sides of your family. Then find out about the genetic history of your people in the same way as you research the genealogy or family history—through reading articles on the molecular genetics history of your ethnic group. You can also talk to relatives and even trace each ancestor's medical histories as far back as oral history or written records take you.

How can you use DNA testing information together with oral histories, diaries, military and court records? You can do online genealogy searches.

Consider looking at any other family memorabilia such as photographs or paintings, even crafts made in the past. Oral history, DNA testing, and genetic history work together with written, medical, and oral family history. Consider the times and background of the dates.

Search the industrial revolution era or before up to the present. What conditions did the person you're searching live under—agricultural or industrial? Was the family confined to a tiny apartment in an urban setting or on a farm? Once you receive the results of DNA testing, you'll have a collection of sequences. Now is your chance to learn how to interpret those sequences by asking questions on the DNA mailing lists and reading up on the subject of what the sequences mean in plain words.

To find out where to get your questions answered about interpreting the sequences, first check with the company that tested your DNA as various labs use different markings. Then contact the message board at Roots Web.com and subscribe to the genealogy digest known as GENEALOGY-DNA-D. You can subscribe to the mailing list and get frequent email, or just the digest, or read the messages at the Web site.

There, you may ask your questions about how to interpret your own sequences or others. To subscribe to GENEALOGY-DNA-D, send a message to GENEALOGY-DNA-D-request@rootsweb.com that contains in the body of the message the command subscribe and no other text. No subject line is necessary, but if your software requires one, just use subscribe in the subject, too.

To contact the GENEALOGY-DNA-D list administrator, send mail to GENEALOGY-DNA-admin@rootsweb.com. Your first step is to ask the company who tested your DNA to tell you how to interpret your sequences. Most companies have a frequently asked questions section on the Web site, and others ask to be emailed questions.

Are you interested in researching, collecting information, scrap booking, genealogy, or writing about family histories or your genetic history? How can you create a time capsule for future generations of printouts of part of your DNA or mtDNA or Y chromosome sequences?

What will future generations do with this information? Can it help unite people who are distant or close relatives or those with the same common ancestor in the very distant past? Family historians and genealogists now have a new branch of genealogy to learn—molecular family history.

There are several excellent books written on how to interpret DNA tests for people without a science background. See the bibliography at the back of this book. I particularly found Alan Savin's book very informative in bringing together DNA testing knowledge to genealogists.

Alan Savin of Maidenhead, England, is author of the 32-page book, DNA for Family Historians (ISBN 0-9539171-0-X). See the Web site: http://www.savin.org/dna/dna-book.html.

This excellent book that I highly recommend explains and explores in layman's language how family historians-genealogists can use DNA research and test results for family history research. The book also has case studies and makes genetic theory easier to understand by those without a background in genetics. It discusses the practicality of DNA testing for family historians as genetics joins genealogy. And it includes discussion of some of the problems of using DNA testing as a tool for family history research.

What I like about this book is that it's written at a reading level that is clear to understand without a science background. And the reader will find a good introduction, historical background, explanation of DNA fingerprinting, mitochondrial DNA testing, Y chromosome DNA testing (for males), collecting and analyzing DNA, future developments, and an excellent bibliography that includes Web sites, magazine articles, and books. So when I contacted Alan Savin by email, he related to me his story of how he introduced genetics into genealogy.

"I believe I was the first family historian in the world to use DNA for genealogical research back in 1997," says Alan Savin. "I originated the phrase 'genetic genealogy'. Realizing its potential, I wished to share this with everybody, hence the writing of the book. It is still selling well, especially in the USA, with orders being received worldwide. I have been approached recently for the book to be translated into German. It has been well received and recommended by a spectrum of reviewers from many genealogical publications, DNA testing companies themselves, e.g. Family Tree DNA and the media, e.g. the BBC."

"As stated in its introduction 'one of my primary aims is to explain this area of genetics in a language easily understood by a genealogist or any lay person'. Further books are planned in the series to develop the themes."

Savin says, "I could be said to be the father of genetic genealogy and I have seen my idea grow with the help of others. I keep a close watch on its development, behind the scenes, and look forward to seeing the science reach its maturity."

Aside from reading books on DNA, what else can a family historian do when there are no records to be found? Hobbyists and professional genealogists who wish to extend their family trees by confirming a link where no conventional source records exist would be interesting in having their DNA tested. Sometimes DNA tests may be used to determine whether a person is part of a larger group of people: for example, Jews will be able to confirm they are of Cohanim lineage. DNA tests are excellent for individuals who want to perform surname-based family tree reconstruction projects.

An excellent article containing another version of the quote below (used with permission) titled, "Tangled Roots? Genetics Meets Genealogy" by Kathryn Brown appeared in the publication, <u>Science,</u> 1 Mar 2002.

Commenting on the role of DNA testing companies, Peter Underhill, a molecular anthropologist at Stanford University admits, "My concern is that people comprehend the relatively low level of resolution offered by these tests. Because the tests analyze relatively few markers along Y DNA or mtDNA, millions of people may share a given molecular profile. I think these companies have a role to play, as long as the science is done well."

Terry Melton, PhD is President/CEO/Laboratory Director of Mitotyping Technologies, LLC, 1981 Pine Hall Drive, State College, PA 16801. "The most important contribution of this science to genealogy is the ability of mtDNA to trace the maternal line long distances throughout a family tree," says Dr. Melton. "My favorite pedigree is one from a paper by Sigurdardottir (*American Journal of Human Genetics* 66:1599) showing fifteen generations of an Icelandic family where living individuals typed from extreme tips of the family (whose ancestral female dates back to 1560) have the same mtDNA profile.

"In addition, mtDNA can sometimes be used to illuminate ethnic ancestry (in a very general way). Mitochondrial DNA types are correlated with the region of the world where the ancestral lineages originate. There have been dozens of scientific papers written on this subject.

"Unlike Y chromosome typing, which should follow the patriline (and family name), mitochondrial DNA is more difficult to correlate with recorded genealogy, since female names are lost in marriages," Melton explains. "However, the possibility remains that if a family can locate two (even very distant) maternal relatives in their tree, the mtDNA typing can confirm the matrilineal connection."

In addition to checking DNA test results with databases and tables on the World Wide Web or in other records, the family historian can compare results and read further about DNA to learn more.

Family members who have their DNA tested also can also track lineages and more recent genealogy by looking at the tell-tale clues that old, antique photos offer as well as use old and new city directories that list people who may not even have had a telephone.

Marjorie Rice rescues old family photos from antique stores and flea markets using the skills and sharp eye of a genealogy researcher to get them back into the hands of family members. An article about her work is on the Web at
http://www.ancestry.com/library/view/news/articles/6590.asp

She looks on the back of the photos to see whether there are family names and/or photographer imprints on the front. She posts the names and locations on surname message boards on the Internet. To date, she has restored 409 photos to family members. See article about her work at: http://www.ancestry.com/library/view/news/articles/6590.asp .

Besides putting dozens of family photos from the early 20th century in my own computer database by scanning and saving, I wrote to various genetic scientists, physicians, and researchers in the field of evolutionary biology and genetics for their opinions regarding the application and use of DNA testing for family historians and genealogists, even for people who want to track and record their own lineages, family trees not only by surname, but by DNA to find out what they can.

Some people are puzzled when "and wife" is listed instead of a female and her maiden name on documents. And with women for hundreds of years taking their father's or husband's surname, doors can open to researching female lines when mtDNA is tested.

Ancient ancestry in female lineages may be traced somewhat by mtDNA. It is inherited by women and passed on to their daughters. Y chromosomes are inherited by men and passed on to their sons. Both show us clues to ancient ancestry or ethnicity even in some small ways that show expansions and migrations of people across geographic distances for thousands of years. Mutation rates and genetic drift due to isolation of small communities show the researcher where the people had sought refuge and how they expanded in clines or gradients of genes.

Where the genes are most diversified shows researchers a clue to where the genes originated rather than where they might be today. Where the genes look alike or very close, shows the people have migrated to an area only recently in the eons of time.

What are various geneticists' and genome scientists' opinions of DNA testing for genealogy research? Richard Villems, MD, Dr. Sci, head of the Department and Professor of Evolutionary Biology at the Institute of Molecular and Cell Biology, Tartu University, Tartu, Estonia, replied to my question by email, noting that, "The answer is straightforward and short: yes, DNA 'testing' is a very powerful method for genealogy research—specifically so as far as maternally inherited mitochondrial BSA and paternally inherited Y chromosome, are concerned.

"Although the current practical use is, technically speaking, far from a possible state-of-art level in case of mtDNA, the latter is, if a full sequence of mtDNA is analyzed, a very precise tool to resolve genealogy in a phylogenetically correct way already. As far as Y chromosome is involved, it would be even more so, because Y chromosome is huge compared to mtDNA—some 60 millions of nucleotides compared to about 16,500 in mtDNA. However, realistically speaking, it would take a huge technological effort to reach a stage where a phylogenetic resolution would be "final"; we are just at the beginning of a long way.

"In theory, even a son will differ from his father, in average, in a few Y-chromosomal mutations—therefore the ideal resolution would indeed allow reconstructing the biological history of this chromosome in minute details. At present, this time is still far away because of an enormous cost of such a work. Nevertheless, the fact that we do know what is possible, one may predict that any man can calculate how exactly he is related to, say, to his contemporary PM of the country—or, say, to the Secretary General of the Chinese Communist Party (if that exists at that future time anyway).

"As far as autosomal genes are involved, I am pessimistic—Mendelian segregation and recombination are probably too powerful in creating noise that such a clear-cut resolution cannot be expected—never.

"Hobbyists and professional genealogists who wish to extend their family trees by confirming a link where no conventional source records exist would be interesting in having their DNA tested. Sometimes DNA tests may be used to determine whether a person is part of a larger group of people: for example, Jews will be able to confirm they are of Cohanim lineage. DNA tests are excellent for individuals who want to perform surname-based family tree reconstruction projects."

Dr. Richard Villems also wrote me this reply, when I inquired about what ethnicities my own mtDNA might reveal, "Your motif in HVS-1 is beyond any reasonable doubt within haplogroup H. Every even slightly experienced in mtDNA researcher knows that although transition in 16356 is a good guess that a particular mtDNA belongs to U4, there are enough 16356 mutations also within H. And what does it mean that 'research showed recently' that 16356C is U4—this is a very well known fact already at least for 4-5 years! But there are exceptions one ought to know as well.

Moreover, this combination you have is well present all over Europe—plenty in Scandinavia, in Estonia as well—but also in Germany and, to make it really a pan-European—also in the Adriatic area as well as in Eastern Europe down to the slopes of the southern Urals, among Turkic-speaking Bashkirs."

I also wrote to another scientist who works with human genetics, Dr. Vincent A. Macaulay, Dept of Statistics, University of Oxford, UK, who replied similarly, "Your sequence (16189-16356-16362) is almost certainly in haplogroup H. I have several exact matches to your sequence in my database which are confirmed as H using other markers in the mtDNA molecule.

"Position 00073 is in HVSII, which is not in the part of the molecule that Oxford Ancestors sequenced. I think they have confused 00073 and 16073 (which is in HVSI) in their reply to you. If you had HVSII sequenced, I would be confident that 00073 would display an "A". The 16356 mutation has happened more than once, so it does not always imply haplogroup U4.

"For your information this sequence has not been observed east of Bulgaria. In my database, there are sequence matches in UK, Spain, Portugal, Germany, Austria and Bulgaria. I hope this helps: I would suggest that you seek further clarification from Oxford Ancestors."

Another scientist in genetics, Dr. Antonio Torroni, Institute of Biochemistry, University of Urbino, Italy, also wrote to me that he found one person from Crete in his mtDNA database with my mtDNA sequences. So where did my own founding female lineage come from and which country represented my direct ancestor—or did all of those countries?

Since only a sample from each country was tested and put in the various database, I wondered whether an ancestor might have been not yet tested, not in the database, and in some geographic area not yet mentioned. The journeys for the founder types have only just begun. What geographic part on Earth, what ethnicity could I ultimately call my own down to the bones? Would I ever find out?

Dr Peter Reed has a PhD in Human Genetics from the University of Oxford and was a pioneer in the use of STR genetic markers in medical research. "To non-enthusiasts genealogy is often considered an obsession with the past," says Reed. "Yet the combination of genetics and genealogy enforces how family history is integral to what we are today." All our ancestors have contributed to our personal genetic makeup, and by examining our own genes we are viewing the DNA of our ancestors.

"Current uses of genetics in genealogy only examine a fraction of our entire
genetic makeup and have largely developed from anthropological research," Reed explains. "However, the driving force of the current 'genetic revolution' has been research into human physiology and psychology, and it is from this work that new applications for genealogy will be developed."

In five to ten years knowledge of our entire personal genetic code will be feasible, and with this knowledge will come an ability to much better understand how our ancestors contributed to our genetic makeup.

"In a few generations from now not only will knowledge of an ancestor's full genetic code be as indispensable for family history as birth and death dates are today, but family history (both genetic and social) will be a vital instrument in personal health care."

* * *

CHAPTER THREE

The Phenomics Revolution: My Positive Experiences with DNA Testing in My Genealogy Search and How This Information Helped Me Write My DNA Detective Novels

"DNA testing is an exquisitely precise tool for answering certain types of genealogical questions, but it is clear that this technique is, and will continue to be, a disappointment to many who see it as a way of leaping over the 'brick walls' in their conventional research," says genealogy researcher, John F. Chandler. "DNA testing is at its best in demonstrating that two people or two lineages are not related within a genealogical time frame."

"When used for the purpose of proving that two people *are* related, it is notoriously often misconstrued. By itself, DNA testing can only show a general relationship, not a specific one," Chandler admits. "For the future, if the field continues to grow, there is some hope that DNA will offer a realistic chance to hunt for relations by looking for exact matches, but the growth will have to be at least three orders of magnitude before this comes to pass."

I wanted to find out more about Ancestry Informative Markers (AIMs) and my own ancestry than only what my mitochondrial DNA (mtDNA) could tell. I wanted to find out the racial percentages in my ancient or recent past. Was I Asian, African, European or what else and in what percentages?

The DNA of the mitochondria is the energy generators transmitted through the egg cells, according to the New York University School of Medicine's Human Genetics Program that offers genetic analysis in various studies. See the Web site at: http://www.med.nyu.edu/genetics/jewishorigins.html. The DNA of the Y chromosome told about male ancestry for males.

Women don't carry the Y chromosome and so are tested for DNA by either their mtDNA for ancestry, or their nuclear DNA. Most DNA testing companies offer mtDNA testing for women and Y chromosome testing for men, and men also have mtDNA, and may have that tested also to learn about their female lineages as well as their male-Y-chromosome lineages.

Some DNA testing companies also offer the racial percentages DNA testing. The racial percentages such as East Asian, Indo European, African, and Native American are DNA tests of Ancestry Informative Markers (AIMs). I wanted to find out what I could about my ancient and recent ancestry that extended beyond records in city directories and other cross-reference files.

Of all the three DNA tests that I took to find out what I could about my unknown ancestry, the DNA test that I found most helpful was the one that looked at the percentages of the various races in my ancestral history. I took The DNAPrint ANCESTRYbyDNA test in order to look at my personal panel of Ancestry Informative Markers (AIMs). "Our test can only indicate to what percentage a person is Native American, African, East Asian and Indo European," says Carrie Castillo, Corporate Communications, DNAPrint genomics. For further information, contact, DNAPrint genomics, Inc. 900 Cocoanut Ave, Sarasota, FL 34236.

The test uses markers that have been characterized in a large number of well-defined population samples. These markers are selected on the bases of showing substantial differences in frequency between population groups and, as such, can tell about the origins of a particular person whose ancestry is unknown.

After the analysis of these Ancestry Informative Markers (AIMs), in a sample of a person's DNA, the probability that a person is derived from any of the parental populations and any of the possible mixes of parental populations is calculated. The population (or combination of populations) where the likelihood is the highest is then taken to be the best estimate of the ancestral proportions of the person. Confidence intervals on these point estimates of ancestral proportions are also being calculated.

For example, the Duffy Null allele (FY*0) is very common (approaching fixation or an allele frequency of 100%) in all sub-Saharan African populations and is not found outside of Africa. So a person with this allele is very likely to have some level of African ancestry.

Knowing the percentage of your races may be one consideration when planning for personalized medicine. How many know the entire history of one's own ancestry? If your parents and grandparents had genetic-related degenerative diseases that are high in certain populations, would you want to know whether you carried genes from a particular ethnic group? I wanted answers to questions such as these because I'm a freelance writer and write novels about DNA.

Ten generations is roughly 250 years and within the time frame of genealogical interest, especially when we are considering the settlement of North America, because they only look at two (2) chromosomes. Y-chromosomal analysis and mtDNA analysis each could only provide information on a very small proportion of a person's ancestors. I went for my third and last DNA test to the AncestryByDNA test because it relies on sequences throughout one's genome. So the results I received from AncestryByDNA said more about a greater number of ancestors. Recently, FamilyTree DNA added AncestryBy DNA's racial percentages test to their offerings.

My goal was to find out what I could for what I could afford, about my ancient ancestry through DNA testing. Perhaps it could tell me something more when oral and written records weren't within reach. The places where my recent relatives lived were mostly unknown to me, and all I could go by was looks as perceived by others based on stereotypes based on cartoons and caricatures. Online database tables told me someone with my matrilineal DNA (mtDNA) lived in Crete. It was as good a starting point as any. So I went out and bought feta cheese for lunch melted on pizza dough.

Then one to four people per thousand with my exact sequences of mtDNA also lived in Scotland and Norway and Siena, Italy (Tuscany) and Turkey and Bulgaria, and Iceland and Austria. What part of the world did my ancestors belong to for any length of time? What would it mean to me other than an ethnic costume for Halloween or a trip to an ethnic restaurant or listening to music of that geographic place?

The first table I researched contained my HVS-1, low resolution sequences of mtDNA. Yet when I had my mtDNA tested for HVS-2, high resolution, different geographical places turned up—the Orkney Islands off the coast of Scotland, France, England, Bulgaria, and Turkey. Well which is the real me—Bulgaria and Turkey or Scotland and Orkney Islands? Grandma had red hair, but that was the paternal side. And red hair is found in all those countries. My hair's dark brown. That could mean anyplace in the world. What could DNA testing tell me that looks did not? My social experiences were based on how others saw me.

For example, at least a dozen times in my life I was stopped and "told" by total strangers what ethnic group I come from and then asked "why did I deviate" from it. When I was twelve, a lady standing next to my mother in a crowded Brooklyn bus pointed to me and shouted, "Why is that Jewish girl wearing a cross?"

Why did that lady choose that particular ethnic group based on so-called stereotypical Ashkenazi "Jewish" looks rather than Greek, Armenian, or Lebanese stereotypical looks? Maybe it was because there were more Ashkenazi Jews in that place than there were Greeks and Armenians or Lebanese?

Was it based on visual stereotypes in print? Or was it herown ethnic group projected on me? What about the man who saw my face as the enemy and already told me what ethnic group I belong to before he beat me up in a public train? He didn't even think of asking first.

How can you tell one ethnic group from another in a crowd or in a train going from one town in New Jersey to the next? Why did my face automatically incite anger or agitation in some people without me doing much other than walking by in front of people or sitting next to them? It wasn't based on color. My freckled face doesn't even tan. Then what was it? The convexity of my nose? My brown hair? How can you tell someone from one country or one religion from another? Can you really tell an Armenian or Greek islands gal from a Polish or Romanian Jew? Does it matter? What would it incite you to kick me in the spine? Or to ask me to my face why I'm trying to "pass" as whatever blends in with the crowd?

As a member (of one high IQ society) from 1978 to 2001, I found myself sitting at a luncheon table when two members, one man and one woman, was so agitated by my name not looking like my face, that I had to show them my ID card to change the subject. They automatically assumed by my face I was Jewish. (Both of them were.)

When they saw the name didn't look like the face, they were astonished. But why was this reaction verbal and necessary to tell me in public at a luncheon gathering. One woman said, "What's a nice Jewish girl like you doing married to Mr. (non-Jewish)? A gentleman next to her said, "I can't believe *that's* your name. You sure don't look Scandinavian. You look Jewish." I couldn't believe at a club meeting in a public restaurant that the conversation would focus on looking at my name on my ID card picture and commenting on my religion or ethnicity.

What brought that up under the umbrella of making general conversation to break the ice? It was the sound of my last name. To them, it didn't look like my face. I still don't get it. What's different about my face? Then the conversation turned to rest of the group discussion the Druid religion.

Perhaps the two Jewish members felt a certain need to connect to me among a table of non-Jews. At that time in the seventies, there was less diversity in that particular California city than there is today. When I returned to another branch of the same club 24 years later, in a different city, the conversation was very different—the stock market. But back then, the conversation ran like this. From a retired dentist kidding around at a club luncheon: "Can't you talk without moving your hands? Try putting your hands in your pockets."

Me: "No. I'm a Greek Islands gal—maybe. And I get nervous when I keep my hands in my pockets." Then I thought. I won't wave my hands. It just raises my blood pressure if I gesture as I talk because that puts emotion behind the words, and it's not great for my health as a genetic introvert with the high anxiety gene.

Years later, when I was in my late fifties, a woman at a bus bench in San Diego said, "You are Jewish and you come from Brooklyn." Both these people were strangers. Yet by the shape of my nose and facial features, they automatically assumed I was an ethnic group whose stereotype caricatures sufficiently motivated them to speak out to the stranger next to them.

When I was thirty and sitting in the student lounge room a blonde woman next to me reading a bible said, "Gee, you look Jewish, but you're so fair." What made these people so openly verbal to a stranger sitting next to them? Comments focused on something about the shape of my nose, dark hair, and my Assyroid skull shape.

So what was in my genes that made people stir that way and comment, or as you'll read on, beat me up for "looking like a particular ethnic group." Oddly, no one asked me what I actually was. They told me, and then proceeded to "act out." My genetic DNA tests that I hoped would reveal my actual identity or mixtures of ethnicities told a new story. That's one of the reasons why I had my DNA tested three times.

Another reason that I wanted to know more about DNA testing for recent and/or ancient origins or at least percentages of the races in my ethnic past beyond what haplogroup in Europe my founding female ancestor camped with (Haplogroup H) 21,000 years ago, was so I could write better DNA Detective novels.

Characters in my novels have genetics-related careers, and they solve forensic DNA problems using clues that I needed to find by reading about molecular genetics and anthropology. My characters solve important problems using DNA clues to answer questions facing DNA researchers.

They work in bioinformatics and solve cold cases using cutting-edge technology, such as in my latest forensic DNA researcher novel, *The DNA Detectives—Working Against Time*, published in paperback by Mystery and Suspense Press, iuniverse, at:
http://www.iuniverse.com/bookstore/book_detail.asp?isbn=0%2D595%2D25339%2D3. Or click on: http://www.iuniverse.com and click on the Bookstore, then look up my book by title or my name.

Being a DNA autodidact became my full-time hobby in the last two years. This year I wrote *The DNA Detectives—Working Against Time*, published in paperback by Mystery and Suspense Press, http://www.iuniverse.com. The search for identity is part of my INFP personality (taking in information and making decisions using my extroverted intuition and introverted feeling) on the MBTI ™.

I spent the decade from 1990 to 2000 exploring my personality type with the Myers-Briggs Type Indicator. Now I needed to go beyond looking at my personality type and which career fit best with my artistic, creative-expression personality and interest in learning science as a senior citizen by reading books at home. Writing diaries as novels had evolved into writing scientific thrillers with romance, mystery, adventure, and suspense.

In the new millennium, with the media popularity of the human genome project, my search for identity through creative writing turned to DNA testing. So reading about DNA remained as my primary hobby. I'm over 61 and have little to do all day but hang around senior centers and go to genealogy club meetings. Reading about the latest in DNA research took me light years beyond genealogy. Of what use is a surname when the name was constantly changed every other generation?

Being a home-based non-driver with little experience in anything more than making use of my Masters degree in English/creative writing and minor in anthropology and illustration by spending the last four decades writing several books a year, with 29 recently published, I put up a Web site at http://dnadetectives.tripod.com. I had two choices on how to spend this decade—knitting at the senior center or writing novels about how people use knowledge of DNA.

My first experience with DNA testing was to have my mtDNA tested to find out anything I could about my ancestry which had been more or less unknown to me, other than having brown hair, hazel eyes, fair skin with a yellow undertone, and freckles. Back in 1964 I was beaten up in a train going from Asbury Park to New York for looking like a particular ethnic group.

Since then I sometimes wondered what is there about my particular facial features that drove someone to beat the heck out of me when I was pregnant and in my twenties. The epithets and body language conveyed to me that I was "crushed" both for looking like a group some people like to insult or strike and for disobeying the passenger's order to wait until the train stopped, even though passing in front of him wouldn't have changed his life in any way.

I wasn't prepared for hate. Someone with fair skin and freckles, green eyes, wasn't told to watch for it. The color of my black wig and the shape of one or two of my facial features set off the rage of epithets hurled at me.

We were both "equal" passengers in a train, and I was showing courtesy by standing at least a few feet from him as I passed in front of him between the cars to return from the restroom to my seat among my family. This wasn't my fault, and I shouldn't have felt that if only I wore a different color wig, I would not have been noticed.

That day I wore my black instead of my blonde wig. I was twenty-two and not really aware of hate crimes or how the color of a wig or the shape of a facial feature might set off a passenger in a commuter train.

Back in 1964 I was riding in a train going from Asbury Park, New Jersey to New York. Out of the blue a middle-aged passenger began tossing loud ethnic epithets at me and demanded that I shouldn't pass between the cars where the restroom was located and the car where my seat was located next to my relatives.

When I ignored his demand to wait until the train stopped in Elizabeth, about a half hour away and tried to pass in front of him to return to my own seat, he grabbed my head, crushing it painfully between his knee and the metal train car door, yelling more ethnic epithets, and kicking me with all his might at the base of the spine. No one came to help. Gee, what if I had been deaf and didn't hear his demand and just went back to my seat because that's what one does after using the john?

Only he called me a name mentioning an ethnic group. It reminded me of the plastic surgeon I met in public when I was fifteen who commented, "Let me take that hump off your nose." (My great grandparents were from the Balkans.)

In any case, that visual familiarity weighed on my mind enough to stir me to find out just how many races or ethnicities I had in my ancestry and why the site of dark hair and Middle Eastern (Neolithic farmer) features would arouse such explosive anger in a European-looking stranger that I had never spoken to, met, touched, or seen, except for my desire to walk past him to a second car and return to my seat from the restroom.

He couldn't have known that I was three months pregnant, married, Unitarian, and American. Not that my ethnicity mattered to anyone on a train, but out of curiosity I wanted to find out where my ancestors had been for the past fifty thousand years.

I've written an article on that travel piece. But getting back to DNA, I saw an announcement on the Web about Oxford Ancestors from http://www.OxfordAncestors.com and had my mtDNA tested.

That's the matrilineal line of ancestry for women. A little cytobrush arrived in the mail. I rubbed the inside of my cheek, and mailed it across the Atlantic to Oxford, England, and two months later, a pretty chart came back with a page on how the mtDNA (mitochondrial DNA) testing was done, a pretty chart linking my mtDNA clan of Helena (or H haplogroup) to everyone else's' in Europe. (A year later the chart changed to how everyone in the world is linked by mtDNA). I also received a printout of the letters of my mtDNA.

The letters were a printout of CGAT, the letters of everyone's DNA, and the chart didn't have the letter of my Haplogroup, but instead, a name given by Oxford Ancestors to the first female ancestor of the H haplogroup clan in Europe, Helena. There was no mention on the chart that Helena was a moniker for the H haplogroup which is one of the most common in Europe, making up about 47% or more of Europeans and 6% of Middle Easterners.

The only clue to my sequences were three little red letters—C showing how I differed in three places from the Cambridge Reference Sequence (CRS) by transitions or mutations of nucleotides, which I was compared against.

I still wanted more—to find what ethnic groups had larger numbers of the same sequences of mtDNA as me. Also, I wanted to know where the most variation occurred, in what part of the world. Perhaps that would give me a clue to the origins. It's not so much how many people today live in an area with your sequences, but how much variation there is that tells you how old your mtDNA is. So I was looking for a founder female, a single person or a coalescence point. For H haplogroup, the coalescence point in Europe had been about 21,000 years. Now I wanted to know, did H arise from a common ancestor somewhere else? If so, where did the someone else come from and was she also an H, or an HV—since H and V split off from HV somewhere and sometime.

Even HV had a common ancestor, pre-HV, somewhere in the Middle East, further back it time. Or did H arise by itself as a mutation in Europe during the height of the Ice Age 21,000 years ago between the coast of SW France and N. Spain's Pyrenees?

The printout of letters didn't mean much to me then. I needed sequences for mutations written in numbers. I found the sequences numbers by asking at one of the genealogy and DNA mailing lists on the Web whether anyone could tell the sequences in numbers from my printed out letters. All I had were the three mutations in red—three "C" letters.

So to answer in part these questions, I wrote to an acquaintance at the Whitehead Institute at MIT (genomics research division) who told me that the three "C" letters (mutations) could be put on another table that I never received or saw before. This table now had numbered sequences.

The table was available to anyone on the Web. I emailed the acquaintance my low-resolution sequence numbers of the HVS-1.

Now I had at last sequences to compare so I could look up what countries of the world these appeared in presently, even though there was no way to tell whether my particular ancestors lived in any particular location at any time. I looked on the Web at Victor Macaulay's HVS-1 tables at
http://www.stats.ox.ac.uk/~macaulay/founder2000/tableA.html and found that my sequences H haplogroup mtDNA of 16189C, 16356C, and 16362C all showed a mutation from T to C and were found with that transition on the table to appear in Spain, England, Austria, and Bulgaria.

Any place else? I emailed an mtDNA research team member, Kristiina Tambets, Estonian Biocentre and Department of Evolutionary

Biology, Tartu University, Tartu, Estonia, who took part in a research study appearing in an article that I read in *Archaeogenetics*, a book published by The McDonald Institute Monographs, edited by Colin Renfrew and Katie Boyle, and Tambets emailed me several sequences, including mine, from her unpublished database.

The few sequences she sent me from her unpublished database classified my sequences as H2b, but she emphasized that I should be cautious as the material was not published. And my sequences in her database of thousands also included other countries listed under H2b, which included my sequences, (a division of haplogroup H).

The sequences listed as well countries that were found to contain at least one or more persons with my HVS-1 sequences, such as: Bashkortostan, Turkey, Crete, Croatia, Albania, Hungary, Portugal, Germany, Iceland, Spain, Norway, Sweden, Komi (Finland group) as well as the others listed on the Web on Macaulay's tables.

The number of samples obtained from each country also was listed in each of the database sequences or tables that I studied. Victor Macaulay's mtDNA (mitochondrial DNA) tables also are on the Web at: http://www.stats.ox.ac.uk/~macaulay/founder2000/tableA.html

My acquaintance from MIT whom I met from Internet correspondence on a mailing list of interest to people working with DNA, wrote that I was probably close to Bulgar/Turk or Karelian or a mixture of all three, when he looked at my sequences back in 2001. He didn't say how he came to that conclusion. However, he asked me to look at all my sequences when searching the tables online.

I assume that the sequences might have shown up among these ethnic groups. So I didn't really learn the process of how he found it out. My research showed England, Spain, Austria, and Bulgaria on Macaulay's tables online. So I needed to learn much more about how to look up sequences on tables that are on the Web for all to access.

If I removed the 189, a fast-mutating site, and only looked at 356 and 362, then it fit well into Karelia, Bulgaria, or Turkey. The 356 mutation, fit with Armenia. But what if I looked at all my sequences? Then other countries were on the tables.

In 2001, I received a certificate from Oxford Ancestors saying I was a Helena (haplogroup H). I thought this was awesome, because I was reared thinking I was in ancient times, at least in part Middle Eastern or from the Caucasus mountains, where U haplogroup is common and H is found at lesser frequencies than in Europe.

In 2002 I received a certificate from Oxford Ancestors saying I was an Ulrike (haplogroup U4). I wrote Vincent Macaulay asking how can one tell which is which with the same mutations?

From his tables and email, he said to find out whether I had a G at position 00073 at HVS-2. He emailed me a note saying that chances are almost certain that I had an A at that position 00073 on HVS-2, if I'd look. Certainly the three mutations I had were in his online database tables. An A at position 00073 of HVS-2 would make me H haplogroup. A G at position 00073 would make me a U4, but the only way to be sure is to do a high resolution test of the mtDNA for HVS-2.

So I wrote to Dr. Villems from Estonia, where Kristiina Tambets database sequences came from and to Bryan Sykes, from Oxford Ancestors. Bryan Sykes, MA PhD DSc, is Professor of Human Genetics, University of Oxford, and with Oxford Ancestors. He has written several books on the history and geography of human genes, including *The Seven Daughters of Eve* and a book on the sons of Adam, genetically speaking. Anyway, Villems also agreed I'm probably an H, not a U4 (what Oxford Ancestors named Ulrike). The question came up because one of my sequences, 16356C also is found in mtDNA haplogroup U4.

Dr. Sykes and I corresponded by email several times, and Dr. Sykes is most helpful and emailed me on January 15, 2002. He wrote, "David Ashworth from Oxford Ancestors has shown me you message and the replies you received from Drs. Macaulay and Villems about whether your DNA sequence places you in the clade of U4 Ulrike or H Helena.

"David tells me that on your original certificate, issued in August 2000, you were placed in the clan of Helena but that when you were sent a replacement you had become a daughter of Ulrike instead. Of course your actual DNA sequence hadn't changed, but the assignment of you clan had.

It may help if I explain how that is done. Clans are defined by a mixture of two sorts of genetic markers, the variants in the control region sequence and the variants at a number of other sites around the mtDNA molecule now generally called SNPs (short for Single Nucleotide Polymorphisms). These are usually designated as +4643Rsa1 or +11329Alu1 etc as you have pointed out in your messages.

"Vincent's classification on the website and in the papers you refer to contain a complete list of these variants. What they mean is that a restriction enzyme recognises the variation and either cuts or does not cut the DNA at that point. Since your hobby is reading about DNA, I am sure I don't need to explain what a restriction enzyme is. So, take +4643Rsa1. That means the enzyme Rsa1 cuts at base number 4643. The variant -4643Rsa1 means that the enzyme does not cut the DNA.

"Vincent and I, with Martin Richards, spent a great deal of time correlating the control region variants with the SNPs by analysing both on several hundred (it may even have been thousands) of mtDNAs and this was an important part of distinguishing the different clans. On the whole these types of variant are more stable than some of the control region sequence variants but not always and ideally every DNA should be tested for both. However, that would put the price to customers up hugely because each one of the SNPs had to be done separately—although I know that Oxford Ancestors are looking into offering this service.

"But even that would not guarantee completely accurate assignment in every single case. Only sequencing the entire mtDNA circle of sixteen and a half thousand bases at astronomical cost would do that—though even that would not be any good unless you had at your fingertips a database of thousands of other complete sequences with which to compare it and only a handful have been completely sequenced to date. Also, as more work is reported, the evolutionary networks will change.

"What I am getting at is that no system is foolproof. The Oxford Ancestors service, to keep it affordable, only sequences the control region. Then the sequence is compared to a database which holds other sequences which have been examined for SNP variants. If the customers control sequence matches up with one of these then it is assigned to the same clan.

In other cases, where there is not an exact match, the database is searched for close matches or sites which are characteristic of particular clans. In the case of your sequence which has variants from the reference sequence at 189, 356, 362 (we delete the 16 prefix for HVS1) two of the three variants are quite unstable—that means they can mutate back and forth. Position 189 is one of the least stable of all and position 362 is not very far behind. Position 356 is far more stable and is also characteristic of clade U4, whose clan mother is Ulrike. However, it is not completely stable and does crop up in other clans—one of which is Helena.

"So the sequence 189, 356, 362 could be in the clan of Ulrike mutating at the unstable positions 189 and 362 away from the U4 root sequence of 356. Or it could be in the clan of Helena with a rare variant at 356 taking it away from 189, 362.

One way of telling the two apart is to look at the variant at 073. This is actually in HVSII and not HVSI and that was a source of confusion in some of the email exchanges I have read.

"Oxford Ancestors doesn't do the 073 test, as you know, so the sequence was assigned on the balance of probabilities to Ulrike. I have now had a chance to compare the sequence to some new research data of my own from Britain in which we did do the 073 test and found five exact matches which carry A at 073, indicative of clade H. So I think you are probably correct and are indeed a daughter of Helena rather than Ulrike. This means that the mutation at 356 would have occurred on a Helena background rather than the 189 and 362 variants occurring on an Ulrike background.

"That might explain why you were originally issued with a Helena certificate in August 2000. At that time, the service was being sent out from my laboratory before Oxford Ancestors acquired its own premises. That means that whoever did that first assignment, and it may well have been me, did recognize the ambiguous nature of the 356 mutation in that particular sequence but that piece of information was not properly transferred to the new set-up—and that is my fault.

"I must thank you for clarifying the assignment of this particular sequence. It is a changing field and your observation has helped it move on one more stage further. I am sure Dr Ashworth will want to issue a new Helena certificate. And of course, I hope you are pleased to have moved back to your original clan."

* * *

Belonging to Helena's clan sounds more personal that what it means—a member of haplogroup H, presumably one of the Seven Daughters of Eve, the founding "clans" or haplogroups found in Europe in prehistoric times. But even H haplogroup had to have a common ancestor before heading for Europe in the middle of the Ice Age 21,000 years ago. And that ancestor had to come from presumably somewhere in the Middle East.

Haplogroup H is the most frequent cluster in the Middle East and the Caucasus. It's present at a frequency 25 percent. In Europe, it's found much more frequently at around 46 percent. There are more haplogroup H people in Europe than there are in any other part of the world.

The mtDNA haplogroup H represents a female ancestor who lived in the Middle East up to 28,400 years ago. Some surviving daughters then went to Europe, and some stayed in the Middle East. However, the European daughters' mtDNA with Haplogroup H have an "age estimate" of only up to 21,400 years. So the arrival of or mutation to H in Europe began more recently in Europe than it did in the Middle East. Yet today there are more Europeans with haplogroup H than there are in the Middle East with the same matrilineal lines of mtDNA haplogroup H.

Other mtDNA haplogroups of female lineages are much older, if we look at mtDNA coalescence times and founder effects. For example, mtDNA haplogroups T and J both date to around 50,000 years before the present in the Middle East, but more recent dates in Europe.

Haplogroup J is found today at its highest frequency in Arabia, making up 25 percent of the Bedouin and Yemeni population. It's also found in Europe, also a more recent arrival. Perhaps mtDNA haplogroup J entered Europe around 10,000 years ago or less, probably with the agricultural revolution of the Neolithic age, after the last Ice Age ended around 12,500 years ago.

The oldest mtDNA in Europe is the female lineage of U mtDNA haplogroup. It's around 50,000 years old in the Middle East, perhaps around 45,000 years ago in Europe, and from U comes many sub divisions such as European-specific U5, North African U6, and Indian U2i, all showing an origin of around 50,000 years ago. The first female lineage out of East Africa into the Middle East was L3, but mtDNA haplogroup U also followed out of Northern Africa and went to Europe as well as most of the Middle East, where it's found today.

An interesting theory is that 50,000 years ago, the route from Northern Africa was closed until 44,000 years ago, so people coming from Asia or Africa into Europe through the Middle East had to come from India across the southern route until the route from the Middle East opened up to get to Europe, and that was around 44,000 years ago.

At that time the Fertile Crescent around what is today Iraq opened up as well as the Levant. By then, people could use a northern route across the Bosphorus from Turkey to Greece and enter Europe. Those in what is today Greece then would have gotten trapped in the Balkans by 25,000 years ago, unless they made it to the refugiums in southwestern France and northwestern Spain near the Mediterranean and at the foot of the Pyrenees. Some made it.

That's why we have the wonderful cave paintings of large animals in southwestern France, particularly the Dordogne valley. Art bloomed when the Ice Age was raging at its maximum and the open tundra or fields of grass was a steppe for animals and hunters.

As soon as the Ice Age ended and forests took over most of Europe, the wonderful art subsided into a dark age that began around 12,000 years ago. Then the early farmers came up from the Middle East. They now make up about 20 percent of Europe's population, and the idea of farming caught on during the next few thousand years. There was an agricultural frontier that separated hunters from farmers, and it lasted thousands of years.

What puzzled me is why today H haplogroup is nearly missing from the Arabian Peninsula. What made it leave, the changing climate or low population frequency? For more information I turned to an excellent article titled "Tracing European Founder mtDNAs" by Richards, et al published in the *American Journal of Human Genetics*, 67:1251-1276, 2000. I read about mtDNA haplogroup V, which appears to have expanded in Europe around 13,000 years ago. Then I re-read Bryan Sykes's book, *The Seven Daughters of Eve*. It was time to take the next step.

So I went to Family Tree DNA for more information. I had my HVS-2 (high resolution) mtDNA tested to find out more about what my ancestry might be and whether I was a U4 or an H haplogroup. The two single female ancestors who founded H and U4 in prehistoric times came from different parts of Eurasia.

Family Tree DNA sent two small felt-tipped serrated pads with a push stick that pushes the felt pad from the holder into a small vial of preservative solution. I brushed the inside of my cheek several times, put the two pads into the two tiny vials of solution, and sent it back. I had a little difficulty poking the stick to drop the pads, and in the end had to pull the pads firmly from the sticks and drop them into the vials with my fingers. (I washed my hands first.)

Family Tree DNA tested more base pairs. I found that indeed there was an A at position 00073 in HVS-2, just like Victor Macaulay told me I'd probably find if I looked. That made me a member of H mtDNA haplogroup. Family Tree DNA also found a new transition to the letter C at position 16519. Family Tree DNA tested 540 base pairs as compared to the 400 tested at Oxford Ancestors, which is close to the minimum that needs to be tested to find out one's mtDNA haplogroup results.

Bennett Greenspan of Family Tree DNA emailed me an answer to my inquiry of what question he would like to see answered in a book on genealogy through DNA testing. *"It would be to explain the direct line of descent...male to male to male, with no mixing of the genders. That's what people seem to have a hard time with."*

What I learned from email correspondence from Family Tree DNA is that my mtDNA won't tell me when the last mutation on a string happened, but H haplogroup in its form as H haplogroup appears on the CRS (Cambridge Reference Sequence) without all the mutations that I have occurring over thousands of years of evolution, is a little over 20,000 years old. (I visualized H as the sequence of the Cro-Magnons of the Mesolithic caves of SW France and Northern Spain.)

Could my ancestors have painted that fine art work on caves at Lascaux or Altamira during the height of the Ice Age? Since then my mtDNA has mutated away from the Cambridge Reference Sequence (CRS), and perhaps the last mutation that occurred in my HVRsequence happened 2-10,000 years ago. Should I look to Europe or the Levant for my founding matrilineal line?

And I wish there was a way to also see what ethnicities my patrilineal line also contributed. I don't have the Y chromosome to trace the Adams in my family, but can a test of percentages of races give me any clue? What tests were within my budget?

Therefore every person I find that matches me exactly on HVR-1 is a nice clue because I am closer to them then to any one else on the direct female side. I like the way Family Tree signs "email me anytime" at the end of each email address. Response time was fast, and my questions were answered.

So I'm thankful for all this information I found useful and practical. They have databases, search engines, and surname projects. Yet I still needed to find out more about what races are in my ancestry. I moved on and found another DNA testing company that even has a chat room.

There are about 3 billion DNA letters (technical name: "base pairs") in human DNA. You can picture these letters as beads on a keychain, each one labeled with an A, C, G, or T. The letters stand for adenine, cytidine, guanine, and thymidine, always referred to as A,C,G, and T. These nucleotide bases are joined together, one after the other like a molecular string of pearls called DNA (deoxyribonucleic acid).

Oxford Ancestors tested only 400 of my HVS-1 sequences. Family Tree DNA tested 540 and found a new mutation or transition16519C in HVS-1. Then when I had HVS-2 tested at Family Tree DNA, I found the transitions also were very common on the CRS and were 309.1C, 315.1C, and deletions at 523- and 524-. Any mutations I had that showed up in my HVS-2 results were more common in the population, and the rare sequence was on the CRS.

I looked up HVS-2 sequences on Victor Macaulay's tables on the Web and found additional countries such as Orkney Islands off the coast of Scotland, Norway, Turkey, Bulgaria, Scotland, and England matching my HVS-2 results. So far, I had no clue as to whether my maternal line was European or Middle Eastern or both. You have to look at HVS-1 and HVS-2 together and not look at them separately when you are trying to find out your nearest common ancestor.

Since my family is so multicultural, I wanted to find out what the DNA said. Family Tree DNA had a database and a name search, but I wasn't able to get into the database or understand what I had to do to check for matches with similar names, but I was very happy with the results.

Now I had low and high resolution mtDNA. That still wasn't enough. There was no way I could afford to have the entire genome checked.

Some Web sites say they will check the whole genome for ancestry or other for a fee that I couldn't afford. Some people want their whole genome done for medical reasons or to make sure medicine is matched to their personal genome.

In a few years, perhaps anyone can have his or her nuclear DNA and entire genome checked for ancestry or to match the right diets or medicines to individual genetic situations. Right now, a whole genome check is priced in the thousands at some sites and at varying prices too high for me.

Also, what I learned from Family Tree DNA, that I never found out from Oxford Ancestors, is that when I had the HVR-2 tested, Family Tree had included some very fast moving, potentially unstable markers to attempt to break down the time when I find a match on HVR-1. This new information helped me move forward in my research for my own ancestry through DNA, something I heard couldn't be done yet, (other than in the distant past.) Yet I was getting closer. Now it was time to move on to the percentages of races that are found in my DNA.

That's when I turned to a BioGeographical Ancestry test from AncestryByDNA. It's a company that recently presented a complex genetics classifier for personalized medicine. AncestryByDNA's CEO is Dr. Tony Frudakis, of DNAPrint genomics, Inc. 900 Cocoanut Ave, Sarasota, FL 34236941-366-3400941-952-9770 fax tfrudakis@dnaprint.com. The

Web site is at http://www.dnaprint.com/. The Web site for testing ancestry such as percentages of various races is located at: www.ancestrybydna.com. They even have a chat room.

DNA testing is about personalized medicine as well as finding out about ancestry and other genetic-related questions. It's also about an informatics platform for genotype pattern recognition.

Here's your gateway to understanding the genetic basis for complex trait determination. DNA testing is about looking at pioneers in the emerging field of post-human genome phenomics. By putting the genomics puzzle together, you become part of the phenomics revolution with ancestry testing or other genotyping services. It's about research on individual genetic responses to certain medications as much as about finding your ancient or racial percentage ancestry.

From the DNA kit I was sent with printed information, I mailed in a DNA sample obtained from rubbing a soft piece of felt inside my cheek on a felt-tipped, serrated swab, which I air-dried and placed in an addressed return envelope and mailed back to DNA Print genomics and asked to be tested for percentages of various racial groups such as African, East Asian, European, and Native American.

Some post offices don't want you to mail biological material, such as DNA. Most post offices, though allow you to put the envelope in a regular mail box, since it only required two first-class stamps to return, weighing around two ounces or less. The envelope contained a signed form with my address so my printed out results could be returned.

You can also get your results by email. To be safe, I placed the return envelope with the two swabs inside of another mailing envelope in case a mailing machine cut a hole in the self-addressed return envelope containing my two pieces of felt with my DNA on it from inside my cheek. If you air-dry the DNA on the small felt tip before you put it in the envelope, you won't get saliva wetting inside of the mailing envelope.

When checking for racial percentages from each parent, the DNA testing goes beyond only testing the mtDNA for women and Y chromosome and/or mtDNA for men. Those results are limited to only a very small number of your ancestors in your ancient past, such as your female founders for mtDNA (women) or Y chromosome and mtDNA for my ancestors who lived perhaps in Ice Age refugiums thousands of years ago.

The test for racial percentages relies on sequences throughout your genome, so a DNA testing company can say more about a greater number of ones ancestors. That's why I went to the BioGeographical Ancestry (BGA) test. More companies are offering it, but I saw it first at ancestrybydna.com. BioGeographical Ancestry (BGA) is the term given to the biological or genetic component of race.

I was looking for what the BGA offered—a simple and objective description of my ancestral origins in terms of the major population groups such as: Native American, East Asian, Indo-European, and sub-Saharan African. BGA estimates represent the mixed nature of all of us in current populations.

Most of us have racial mixing in the distant past that we don't know about yet. I wanted to find out because my ancestors lived both in Europe and along the Silk Road in ancient and/or medieval times.

I'm interested in reading about molecular anthropology. I write novels about the work of fictional molecular anthropologists and similar researchers.

My experiences reading in anthropology taught me that anywhere in the world there have been mixing, even among groups isolated for thousands of years. I wanted to find out the percentages of different races I had in my background.

Was I 100 percent Indo-European or only a small percentage, and what other races were in my continuum of ancestors recently and in the distant past? What type of ancestry contributed to my inability to tan, but get freckled and wrinkled in the sun or look yellowish in the summer compared to someone with pinkish skin. Cosmeticians call my type "an autumn" because orange, rust, and forest green colors are becoming to my hazel eyes and dark brown hair. Honey-colored rouge looks good on me. And peach, not pink goes well with my coloring.

My search for self-identity motivated me to take these types of DNA tests. Maybe that's why I'm a novelist today, writing mystery novels about DNA scientists. Reading molecular anthropology books are my favorite hobby along with genealogy by DNA and looking into the past is a great inspiration to my novel-writing career now that I'm a senior citizen. Any way, my haplogroup is H, sequences HVS-1 at 16189C, 16356C, 16362C, 16519C and HVS-2, sequences at 263G, 309.1C, 315.1C, 523-, 524-.

All these sequences are very common all of Europe and who knows where else? So, at the present, only the test of racial percentages gave me some clue to where my ancestors might have come from way back when and maybe more recently, too. The phenomics revolution is new and fascinating.

The reasons why you would look at more of your genome is useful, not frightening. And all the new ways to look at your genome are becoming more personalized and relevant. With phenomics, the future moves towards personalized medicine. And DNA testing offers a more personalized genealogy for us history buffs and novelists.

Let's say you tested your mtDNA to find your female lineage, but you want to look up female relatives and don't know their maiden names. My own great grandmother's death certificate didn't list a maiden name. The next step would be to look at her marriage certificate.

I could also look at the City Directory for a particular city in 1889 to see where she lived, looking first under her father's name. I could try the US Census records for 1890 also in that city. My grandparents were small children at that time living in a large house and farm in upstate New York, and all I know to begin my search is my great grandmother's first name and her father's last name, and I have my mtDNA, female lineage high and low resolution sequences.

Those would be the same in my great grandmother as in my present grand daughter. The mtDNA stretches back to a single female founder 21,000 years ago in Europe and further back in time, the usual cereal belt. I know my sequences are quite popular in Crete.

City Directories often list maiden names and the names of all residents living in a home, particular before homes had telephones. Where else can you look on the Web to start besides the usual beginning genealogy Web sites? You might order marriage certificates or death certificates as well as birth certificates to find maiden names.

The National Center for Health Statistics in Hyattsville, Maryland is also on the World Wide Web at:
http://www.cdc.gov/nchs/howto/w2w/newyork.htm. For example, to view an address where to write to in order to purchase a copy of a marriage certificate for New York State, the Web site will help provide information as to where to write to in order to purchase copies of marriage licenses for New York, for example, from the year 1880 forward.

For other states, check the Web site at The National Center for Health Statistics under each state. You can also search foreign countries for records. You could also look at the Ellis Islands records, if a relative came to Ellis Island, and even view a picture of the ship at the Ellis Island Online Web site at: http://www.ellisisland.org/.

One good place to start is http://www.cdc.gov/nchs/products.htm for publications and products. Click on http://www.cdc.gov/nchs/nvss.htm for Vital Statistics. Click here http://www.cdc.gov/nchs/releases/96facts/mardiv.htm for marriage and divorce statistics.

* * *

CHAPTER FOUR

Companies That Bring the Power of DNA Technology to Your Home

The DNA Testing Companies of Interest to Family Historians and Genealogists

The Power of DNA Technology in Every Home. This is the slogan of the GeneTree DNA Testing Center that supplies DNA testing applications directly to the consumer. "We would like to demonstrate how we provide the science of DNA analysis applications directly to the consumer, allowing them to conduct their own research projects in the comfort of their own home," says Terrence C. Carmichael, MS, founder of GeneTree DNA Testing Center.

"By examining the Autosomal STRs, Y-chromosome STRs and mtDNA sequence analysis and RFLP, GeneTree is helping people (such as genealogists, anthropologists, and just those generally interested) uncover their deep ancestral migration patterns, establish biological relationships with relatives 1-50 generations apart, and uncover the mysteries of past and present relationships. These services are wonderful, and prove to be of great value to the consumer, whether it is for immigration purposes, assistance with genealogy or anthropology research, or for answering the simplest of questions, such as 'are you my father?'"

After receiving his MS degree, Carmichael went on to receive a Professional Designation in Marketing and Sales from UCLA. Terry has worked at the DNA laboratory bench for 4 years and spent 9 years providing Product Development, Technical Consulting, and Marketing for the DNA purification industry, working for companies such as Bio-Rad and QIAGEN. In 2000, Carmichael co-authored a book titled, "How to DNA Test your Family Relationships".

Having started 2 successful businesses, Terry is a visionary. He has applications submitted for 2 separate patents; one for applying DNA profiles to identification cards and the other for a new high-throughput DNA purification product held by Bio-Rad Laboratories. Below are the Web sites for some of the products offered by GeneTree DNA Testing Center.

GeneTree Products:
http://www.genetree.com/servlet/moonshine/goto?page_url=/products/productgroups.jsp
Y-Chromosome Information:
http://www.genetree.com/servlet/moonshine/goto?page_url=/products/product.jsp&id=7
mtDNA Information:
http://www.genetree.com/servlet/moonshine/goto?page_url=/products/product.jsp&id=8
Native American Assessment:
http://www.genetree.com/servlet/moonshine/goto?page_url=/products/product.jsp&id=20

Biography: Terrence C. Carmichael, MS
Terrence Carmichael, MS
(888) 404-GENE (ext. 207)

****

GeneTree DNA Testing Center
3150 Almaden Expressway, #203
San Jose, CA 95118-1253
Phone: (888) 404-GENE/(408) 723-2670
Fax: (408) 723-2671 http://www.genetree.com/
****

The Power of DNA Technology in Every Home

FamilyTreeDNA

Here's how genealogy and DNA testing interacted together for the Craycraft Surname Project from FamilyTreeDNA. The Craycraft DNA project involves the surnames: Cracraft, Craycraft, Cracroft, Craycroft, and Craecraft. For purposes of this article, sent to me by FamilyTreeDNA, the use of the surname Craycraft refers to all the possible spellings noted above, unless otherwise indicated.

The surname first appears as Cracroft, in Hogsthorpe, England in the early 1200's with one Walter de Cracroft son of Humphrey Fitz Walter. It is later found in Hackthorn, England in the early 1600's, and today a Cracroft family still resides in Hackthorn Hall. Currently there are about 10,000 people, with this surname, and the surname is found in the following countries: England, USA, Canada, and New Zealand.

The first known emigrants to the Americas with this surname were John Cracroft and his wife Ann who emigrated from Lincolnshire, England in about 1665. The passenger list has John and Ann recorded as Creacroft or Creacraft. Today the descendents of John and Ann mostly spell their surname as Craycroft. Later, Joseph Cracraft/Cracroft came to the America's circa 1702 from Lincolnshire, England. He had 5 sons.

The objectives of the DNA project for phase I were the following:
1. Verify the documented genealogy research for the Joseph line in the US
2. Verify the documented genealogy research for the John line in the US
3. Determine whether the US Craycrafts are related to any England Cracrofts.

To meet the objective of verifying documented genealogy research, multiple participants were required due to the many branches between now and the identified most distant ancestor. The Lines tested are shown below, labeled by the most distance ancestor's name.

Joseph Cracraft, born Lincolnshire, England: Descendents of 3 of his 5 sons. John Cracroft, emigrated from Lincolnshire, England in about 1665 Cracroft family residing in Lincolnshire England, descendents of Walter de Cracroft.

The results from Phase I:
1. The documented genealogy of the descendents of 3 sons of Joseph was verified. A search continues for descendents of the 2 other sons.
2. The documented genealogy of John's descendents was verified.
3. The DNA results of Joseph and John's descendents matched as well as these DNA results matched those of the present day Lincolnshire family of Cracroft.

The surprises uncovered:
1. It was rumored that a female ancestor had a male child out of wedlock, and the child assumed the family surname. This was confirmed by the descendents in this branch having different DNA.
2. An adoption or non paternity event was discovered when a descendant's DNA results did not match. This event was confirmed by testing descendents from a branch earlier in the line, which did match the Craycraft DNA results.

A Phase II of the project is planned.

===================================
Spot Light: Austin Research Validation
===================================

Validating research with DNA testing: Descendents of John Austin, JR (1726-1795)

Records in the US in the 1700's are scarce, and researching in this time period is very difficult. After 26 years of research, there was a preponderance of circumstantial evidence that showed that William Austin (b. Bet. 1750—1760, Hallifax County, Virginia or Surry County, North Carolina) was a son of John Austin, Jr. (born 14 Sep 1726, James City County, Cornwall Parish, Virginia (now Halifax & Pittsylvania).

After 26 years of exhaustive research, the researchers turned to DNA testing to find the answer. The objective of the testing was to determine whether the circumstantial evidence from research showing that William was a son of John Austin, Jr. could be proven or disproved.

To accomplish this objective, two participants were selected. One participant was a documented descendent of William Austin. The other participant was a documented descendent of one of the sons of John Austin, Jr., Isaiah. The results of the DNA test confirmed the research.

===================================
Spot Light: Roper Surname Project
===================================

Objective: Determine if any of the Roper Lines are related. There are many Roper Lines in the US and England that can not be connected by documents. For Ropers with ancestors who resided in new Kent County Virginia, the courthouse fires destroyed all records before 1864, severely limiting the ability to trace a family tree past 1864 and connect with any other Roper Line. To date, 25 participants have been tested. The geographic representation of these participants include:

18 US
2 Canada
1 Australia/England
4 UK

The surnames tested are Roper and Rooper. The results to date have exceeded expectations and been a significant contribution to Roper genealogy research. The major results include:
1. The majority of Roper Lines in the US match 24/25 or 25/25. One of these lines can trace their ancestor back to John Roper, born 1611.
2. County Norfolk in England has been identified as the ancestral homeland.
3. Most of the branches of the US Ropers have a different mutation, enabling a branch to be identified by the mutation.

In addition, research was confirmed when a participant who descended from a female Roper did not match, as would be expected. The next phase of the Project involves more testing in England, concentrating on the Counties of Norfolk and Kent, where Ropers from Norfolk migrated.

From CL of Savannah, GA

"I used FamilyTreeDNA for our guys. They do an extra strand, I believe. Our Rosenblaths go back to the 1600's. However when they came to America their name was misspelled many different ways. It was hard to tell who was related to whom. Recently we had a confirmed "Rosenplot" relation in TN, originating in Canada as with my Grandmother who is descended from Rosenplot, submitted his DNA test to see if he was related to an unknown Rosenblath in Shrevesport LA.

"It comes to find out we have several relations, a Robertson who thought they were Scottish because of their name, and several more differently spelled Rosenplots/Rosenblaths. It has brought all of us who were strangers together in a very meaningful way. We share news about our families. Some have been able to 'paper' prove the connection while others are still looking for a few generations old grandfather in the tree we have. It has been great! A lot of new contacts!"

                         *   *   *

CHAPTER FIVE

What is DNA?

"The human genome is about 3 x 109 base pairs long, which would weigh about 40 pg (picograms: 1 pg=10-12 grams) per genome," reports Michael Onken, and this description appears on the science Web site of Ricky J. Sethi, MadSci.ORG Administrator at MadSci.ORG (http://www.madsci.org) at the Washington University School of Medicine, http://www.madsci.org/. "Human cells are diploid, i.e. each contains two copies of the genome, so the nuclear DNA from a human cell would weigh about 80 pg. If we want total cellular DNA, then we need to include mitochondrial DNA (mtDNA).

"The human mitochondrial genome is about 16,000 base pairs long. There are about 10 copies of the genome per mitochondrion, and there are on the order of 1,000 mitochondria per cell. This gives us about 0.2 pg of mtDNA per human cell.

"There are on the order of 1014 cells per adult human, many of which are without nuclei, like skin cells and red blood cells. This would give us just under a kilogram of chromosomal DNA and on the order of a few grams of mitochondrial DNA in the average human body."

(This excerpt is reprinted with permission of Ricky J. Sethi, MadSci.ORG Administrator, at the Washington University School of Medicine. See the Web site at http://www.madsci.org/.)

Knowing how many genes a human has in the future will help not only genealogists and other family and oral historians trace ancestors and keep records of lineages, but physicians will be able to tailor medicines to help people based on how their individual genes react to different elixirs, drugs, natural supplements, herbs, foods, and medicines.

Combined with the knowledge of rainforest tropical plants and their cures, the human genome is headed towards individualization and customization, with an appropriate mixture of food, medicine, or therapy based on one's individual genetic makeup. To the person without a science background, knowing one's genes also is a way to connect people to their common ancestors in the past and to those descendants.

Family history can be researched not only for medical reasons, but for historical reasons, and to show how people are related to one another down through the ages. To understand how DNA testing relates to history and family records, let's look at some basics of genomics such as what are cells and what is DNA. Then we can think about ways we can use the results of DNA tests in the realm of family history.

Credit for the following Primer below and Dictionary at the back of this book is acknowledged to the U.S. Department of Energy Human Genome Program as the source for both and included also here is the U.S. Department of Energy Human Genome Program's Web site for more information on the Human Genome Project and its applications: www.ornl.gov/hgmis.

This document may be cited in the following style: Human Genome Program, U.S. Department of Energy, *Genomics and Its Impact on Medicine and Society: A 2001 Primer*, 2001. For printed copies, please contact Laura Yust at Oak Ridge National Laboratory. Send questions or comments to the author, Denise K. Casey. Site on the Web designed by Marissa Mills. **This primer was prepared by Denise Casey, Human Genome Management Information System, Oak Ridge National Laboratory. You can find this Primer on the Web at:** http://www.ornl.gov/hgmis/publicat/primer2001/1.html and the index to additional publications at: http://www.ornl.gov/hgmis/publicat/primer2001/index.html

Genomics and Its Impact on Medicine and Society: A 2001 Primer (Courtesy of the U.S. Department of Energy Human Genome Program: http://www.ornl.gov/hgmis

The Basics

Cells are the fundamental working units of every living system. All the instructions needed to direct their activities are contained within the chemical DNA (deoxyribonucleic acid).

DNA from all organisms is made up of the same chemical and physical components. The DNA sequence is the particular side-by-side arrangement of bases along the DNA strand (e.g., ATTCCGGA). This order spells out the exact instructions required to create a particular organism with its own unique traits.

The **genome** is an organism's complete set of DNA. Genomes vary widely in size: the smallest known genome for a free-living organism (a bacterium) contains about 600,000 DNA base pairs, while human and mouse genomes have some 3 billion. Except for mature red blood cells, all human cells contain a complete genome.

DNA in the human genome is arranged into 24 distinct **chromosomes**—physically separate molecules that range in length from about 50 million to 250 million base pairs. A few types of major chromosomal abnormalities, including missing or extra copies or gross breaks and rejoinings (translocations), can be detected by microscopic examination. Most changes in DNA, however, are more subtle and require a closer analysis of the DNA molecule to find perhaps single-base differences.

Each chromosome contains many **genes**, the basic physical and functional units of heredity. Genes are specific sequences of bases that encode instructions on how to make proteins. Genes comprise only about 2% of the human genome; the remainder consists of noncoding regions, whose functions may include providing chromosomal structural integrity and regulating where, when, and in what quantity proteins are made. The human genome is estimated to contain 30,000 to 40,000 genes.

Although genes get a lot of attention, it's the **proteins** that perform most life functions and even make up the majority of cellular structures. Proteins are large, complex molecules made up of smaller subunits called amino acids.

Chemical properties that distinguish the 20 different amino acids cause the protein chains to fold up into specific three-dimensional structures that define their particular functions in the cell.

The constellation of all proteins in a cell is called its **proteome**. Unlike the relatively unchanging genome, the dynamic proteome changes from minute to minute in response to tens of thousands of intra- and extra cellular environmental signals.

A protein's chemistry and behavior are specified by the gene sequence and by the number and identities of other proteins made in the same cell at the same time and with which it associates and reacts. Studies to explore protein structure and activities, known as proteomics, will be the focus of much research for decades to come and will help elucidate the molecular basis of health and disease.

* * *

CHAPTER SIX

Human Genome Project

Genomics and Its Impact on Medicine and Society: A 2001 Primer

Reprinted with permission of the US Dept. of Energy, Human Genome Program,
http://www.ornl.gov.hgmis

A Little Bit of History

Though surprising to many, the Human Genome Project (HGP) traces its roots to an initiative in the U.S. Department of Energy (DOE). Since 1945, DOE and its predecessor agencies have been charged by Congress to develop new energy resources and technologies and to pursue a deeper understanding of potential health and environmental risks posed by their production and use.

Such studies have since provided the scientific basis for individual risk assessments of nuclear medicine technologies, for example. In 1986, DOE took a bold step in announcing its Human Genome Initiative, convinced that DOE's missions would be well served by a reference human genome sequence. Shortly there-after, DOE and the National Institutes of Health developed a plan for a joint HGP that officially began in 1990.

Ambitious Goals...

From the outset, the HGP's ultimate goal has been to generate a high-quality reference sequence for the entire human genome and to identify all human genes. Other important goals are to sequence the genomes of model organisms to help interpret human DNA, enhance computational resources to support future research and commercial applications, and explore gene function through mouse-human comparisons.

Potential applications are numerous and include customized medicines, improved agricultural products, new energy resources, and tools for environmental cleanup. The HGP also aims to train future scientists, study human variation, and address critical societal issues arising from the increased availability of personal human genome data and related analytical technologies.

...and Exciting Progress

Although the HGP originally was planned to last 15 years, rapid technological advances and worldwide participation have accelerated the expected completion date to 2003. In June 2000, scientists announced biology's most stunning achievement: the generation of a working draft sequence of the entire human genome. In addition to serving as a scaffold for the finished version, the draft provides a road map to an estimated 90% of genes on every chromosome and already has enabled gene hunters to pinpoint genes associated with more than 30 disorders.

HGP resources have spurred a boom in spin-off sequencing programs on the human and other genomes in both the private and public sectors. To stimulate further research, all data generated in the public sector are made available rapidly and free of charge via the Web.

HGP Spinoff Projects

- **Microbial Genome Project**
  1. www.sc.doe.gov/ober/microbial.html
  2. www.ornl.gov/microbialgenomes/
- **Microbial Cell Project**
  microbialcellproject.org
- **Genomes to Life**
  doegenomestolife.org
- **Environmental Genome Project**
  www.niehs.nih.gov/envgenom/home.htm
- **Cancer Genome Anatomy Project**
  www.ncbi.nlm.nih.gov/ncicgap/
- **SNP Consortium**
  snp.cshl.org

Human Genome Project Goals 1998-2003

Human DNA Sequencing

The HGP's continued emphasis is on obtaining by 2003 a complete and highly accurate reference sequence (1 error in 10,000 bases) that is largely continuous across all human chromosomes. Scientists believe that knowing this sequence is critically important for understanding human biology and for applications to other fields.

A "working draft" of the sequence was completed 18 months ahead of schedule, in June 2000. The achievement has provided scientists worldwide with a road map to an estimated 90% of genes on every chromosome. Although the draft contains gaps and errors and does not yet meet the standard of accuracy outlined above, it provides a valuable scaffold for generating a high-quality reference genome sequence. HGP scientists make human DNA sequence available broadly, rapidly, and free of charge via the Web.

Sequencing Technology

Although current sequencing capacity is far greater than at the inception of the HGP, further incremental progress in sequencing technologies, efficiency, and cost-reduction are needed. For future sequencing applications, planners emphasize the importance of supporting novel technologies that may be 5 to 10 years in development.

Sequence Variation

Although more than 99% of human DNA sequences are the same across the population, variations in DNA sequence can have a major impact on how humans respond to disease; to such environmental insults as bacteria, viruses, toxins, and chemicals; and to drugs and other therapies.

Methods are being developed to detect different types of variation, particularly the most common type called single-nucleotide polymorphisms (SNPs), which occur about once every 100 to 300 bases. Scientists believe SNP maps will help them identify the multiple genes associated with such complex diseases as cancer, diabetes, vascular disease, and some forms of mental illness. These associations are difficult to establish with conventional gene-hunting methods because a single altered gene may make only a small contribution to disease risk.

Functional Genomics
Efficient interpretation of the functions of human genes and other DNA sequences requires that strategies be developed to enable large-scale investigations across whole genomes. A first priority is to generate complete sets of full-length cDNA clones and sequences for human and model-organism genes. Other functional-genomics goals include studies into gene expression and control and the development of experimental and computational methods for understanding gene function.

Comparative Genomics
The functions of human genes and other DNA regions often are revealed by studying their parallels in nonhumans. HGP researchers have obtained complete genomic sequences for the bacterium Escherichia coli, the yeast Saccharomyces cerevisiae, the fruit fly Drosophila melanogaster, and the roundworm Caenorhabditis elegans. Sequencing continues on the laboratory mouse. The availability of complete genome sequences generated both inside and outside the HGP is driving a major breakthrough in fundamental biology as scientists compare entire genomes to gain new insights into evolutionary, biochemical, genetic, metabolic, and physiological pathways.

Ethical, Legal, and Social Implications (ELSI)
Rapid advances in the science of genetics and its applications present new and complex ethical and policy issues for individuals and society. ELSI programs that identify and address these implications have been an integral part of the U.S. HGP since its inception. These programs have resulted in a body of work that promotes education and helps guide the conduct of genetic research and the development of related medical and public policies.

Bioinformatics and Computational Biology
Continued investment in current and new databases and analytical tools is critical to the success of the HGP and to the future usefulness of the data it produces. Databases must adapt to the evolving needs of the scientific community and must allow queries to be answered easily. Planners suggest developing a human genome database, analogous to model organism databases that will link to phenotypic information. Also needed are databases and analytical tools for studying the expanding body of gene-expression and functional data, for modeling complex biological networks and interactions, and for collecting and analyzing sequence-variation data.

Training

Future genome scientists will require training in interdisciplinary areas including biology, computer science, engineering, mathematics, physics, and chemistry. Also, scientists with management skills will be needed for leading large data-production efforts.

See Previous Goals
1998-2003 Third Five Year Plan
1993-1998 Second Five Year Plan
1991-1995 Original HGP Goals

*   *   *

CHAPTER SEVEN

What We've Learned So Far

Genomics and Its Impact on Medicine and Society: A 2001 Primer

Reprinted with permission of the US Dept. of Energy, Human Genome Program,
http://www.ornl.gov.hgmis

Achievement of a Draft Human Genome Sequence

In February 2001, HGP and Celera Genomics scientists published the long-awaited details of the working-draft DNA sequence. Although the draft is filled with mysteries, the first panoramic view of the human genetic landscape has revealed a wealth of information and some early surprises. Papers describing research observations in the journals *Nature* (Feb. 15, 2001) and *Science* (Feb. 16, 2001) are freely accessible.

Although clearly not a Holy Grail or Rosetta Stone for deciphering all of biology—two early metaphors commonly used to describe the coveted prize—the sequence is a magnificent and unprecedented resource that will serve as a basis for research and discovery throughout this century and beyond. It will have diverse practical applications and a profound impact upon how we view ourselves and our place in the tapestry of life.

One insight already gleaned from the sequence is that, even on the molecular level, we are more than the sum of our 35,000 or so genes.

Surprisingly, this newly estimated number of genes is only one-third as great as previously thought and only twice as many as those of a tiny transparent worm, although the numbers may be revised as more computational and experimental analyses are performed.

At once humbled and intrigued by this finding, scientists suggest that the genetic key to human complexity lies not in the number of genes but in how gene parts are used to build different products in a process called alternative splicing. Other sources of added complexity are the thousands of chemical modifications made to proteins and the repertoire of regulatory mechanisms controlling these processes.

The draft encompasses 90% of the human genome's euchromatic portion, which contains the most genes. In constructing the working draft, the 16 genome sequencing centers produced over 22.1 billion bases of raw sequence data, comprising overlapping fragments totaling 3.9 billion bases and providing sevenfold coverage (sequenced seven times) of the human genome. Over 30% is high-quality, finished sequence, with eight- to tenfold coverage, 99.99% accuracy, and few gaps.

High-Quality Version Expected in 2003

The entire working draft will be finished to high quality by 2003. Coincidentally, that year also will be the 50th anniversary of Watson and Crick's publication of DNA structure that launched the era of molecular genetics. Much will remain to be deciphered even then. Some highlights follow from Nature, Science, and The Wellcome Trust philanthropy (an HGP funder).

By the Numbers
- The human genome contains 3164.7 million chemical nucleotide bases (A, C, T, and G).

- The average gene consists of 3000 bases, but sizes vary greatly, with the largest known human gene being dystrophin at 2.4 million bases.
- The total number of genes is estimated at 30,000 to 40,000, much lower than previous estimates of 80,000 to 140,000 that had been based on extrapolations from gene-rich areas as opposed to a composite of gene-rich and gene-poor areas.
- The order of almost all (99.9%) nucleotide bases is exactly the same in all people.
- The functions are unknown for more than 50% of discovered genes.

The Wheat from the Chaff

- About 2% of the genome encodes instructions for the synthesis of proteins.
- Repeated sequences that do not code for proteins (Òjunk DNAÓ) make up at least 50% of the human genome.
- Repetitive sequences are thought to have no direct functions, but they shed light on chromosome structure and dynamics. Over time, these repeats reshape the genome by rearranging it, thereby creating entirely new genes or modifying and reshuffling existing genes.
- During the past 50 million years, a dramatic decrease seems to have occurred in the rate of accumulation of these repeats.

How It's Arranged

- The human genome's gene-dense "urban centers" are composed predominantly of the DNA building blocks G and C.
- In contrast, the gene-poor "deserts" are rich in the DNA building blocks A and T. GC- and AT-rich regions usually can be seen

through a microscope as light and dark bands on the chromosomes.
- Genes appear to be concentrated in random areas along the genome, with vast expanses of noncoding DNA between.
- Stretches of up to 30,000 C and G bases repeating over and over often occur adjacent to gene-rich areas, forming a barrier between the genes and the "junk DNA." These CpG islands are believed to help regulate gene activity.
- Chromosome 1 has the most genes (2968), and the Y chromosome has the fewest (231).

How the Human Genome Compares with Those of Other Organisms

- Unlike the human's seemingly random distribution of gene-rich areas, many other organisms' genomes are more uniform, with genes evenly spaced throughout.
- Humans have on average three times as many kinds of proteins as the fly or worm because of mRNA transcript "alternative splicing" and chemical modifications to the proteins. This process can yield different protein products from the same gene.
- Humans share most of the same protein families with worms, flies, and plants, but the number of gene family members has expanded in humans, especially in proteins involved in development and immunity.
- The human genome has a much greater portion (50%) of repeat sequences than the mustard weed (11%), the worm (7%), and the fly (3%).
- Although humans appear to have stopped accumulating repetitive DNA over 50 million years ago, there seems to be no such decline in rodents. This may account for some of the fundamental differences

between hominids and rodents, although estimates of gene numbers are similar in both species. Scientists have proposed many theories to explain evolutionary contrasts between humans and other organisms, including life span, litter sizes, inbreeding, and genetic drift.

Variations and Mutations

- Scientists have identified about 1.4 million locations where single-base DNA differences (SNPs, see Goals Box: Sequence Variation) occur in humans. This information promises to revolutionize the processes of finding chromosomal locations for disease-associated sequences and tracing human history.
- The ratio of germline (sperm or egg cell) mutations is 2:1 in males vs females. Researchers point to several reasons for the higher mutation rate in the male germline, including the greater number of cell divisions required for sperm formation than for eggs.

Applications, Future Challenges

Deriving meaningful knowledge from the DNA sequence will define research through the coming decades to inform our understanding of biological systems. This enormous task will require the expertise and creativity of tens of thousands of scientists from varied disciplines in both the public and private sectors worldwide.

The draft sequence already is having an impact on finding genes associated with disease. Genes have been pinpointed and associated with numerous diseases and disorders including breast cancer, muscle disease, deafness, and blindness. Additionally, finding the DNA sequences underlying such common diseases as cardiovascular disease, diabetes, arthritis, and cancers is being aided by the human SNP maps generated in the HGP in cooperation with the private sector. These genes and SNPs provide focused targets for the development of effective new therapies.

One of the greatest impacts of having the sequence may well be in enabling an entirely new approach to biological research. In the past, researchers studied one or a few genes at a time. With whole-genome sequences and new automated, high-throughput technologies, they can approach questions systematically and on a grand scale. They can study all the genes in a genome, for example, or all the gene products in a particular tissue or organ or tumor, or how tens of thousands of genes and proteins work together in interconnected networks to orchestrate the chemistry of life.

*　　　　*　　　　*

CHAPTER EIGHT

After the Human Genome Project (HGP), the Next Steps...

Genomics and Its Impact on Medicine and Society: A 2001 Primer

Reprinted with permission of the US Dept. of Energy, Human Genome Program,
http://www.ornl.gov.hgmis

The words of Winston Churchill, spoken in 1942 after 3 years of war, capture well the HGP era: "Now this is not the end. It is not even the beginning of the end. But it is, perhaps, the end of the beginning."

The avalanche of genome data grows daily. The new challenge will be to use this vast reservoir of data to explore how DNA and proteins work with each other and the environment to create complex, dynamic living systems.

Systematic studies of function on a grand scale—functional genomics—will be the focus of biological explorations in this century and beyond. These explorations will encompass studies in transcriptosmics, proteomics, structural genomics, new experimental methodologies, and comparative genomics.

- **Transcriptomics** involves large-scale analysis of messenger RNAs (molecules that are transcribed from active genes) to determine when, where, and under what conditions genes are expressed.
- **Proteomics**—the study of protein expression and function—can bring researchers closer than gene-expression studies to what's actually happening in the cell.

- **Structural genomics** initiatives are being launched worldwide to generate the 3-D structures of one or more proteins from each protein family, thus offering clues to their function and providing biological targets for drug design.
- **Knockout studies** are one experimental method for understanding the function of DNA sequences and the proteins they encode. Researchers inactivate genes in living organisms and monitor any changes that could reveal the function of specific genes.
- **Comparative genomics**—analyzing DNA sequence patterns of humans and well-studied model organisms side by side—has become one of the most powerful strategies for identifying human genes and interpreting their function.

> Medicine and the New Genetics: Gene Testing, Pharmacogenomics, and Gene Therapy

DNA underlies every aspect of human health, both in function and dysfunction. Obtaining a detailed picture of how genes and other DNA sequences function together and interact with environmental factors ultimately will lead to the discovery of pathways involved in normal processes and in disease pathogenesis. Such knowledge will have a profound impact on the way disorders are diagnosed, treated, and prevented and will bring about revolutionary changes in clinical and public health practice. Some of these transformative developments are described below.

Gene Tests

DNA-based tests are among the first commercial medical applications of the new genetic discoveries. Gene tests can be used to diagnose disease, confirm a diagnosis, provide prognostic information about the course of disease, confirm the existence of a disease in asymptomatic individuals, and, with varying degrees of accuracy, predict the risk of future disease in healthy individuals or their progeny.

Currently, several hundred genetic tests are in clinical use, with many more under development, and their numbers and varieties are expected to increase rapidly over the next decade. Most current tests detect mutations associated with rare genetic disorders that follow Mendelian inheritance patterns. These include myotonic and Duchenne muscular dystrophies, cystic fibrosis, neurofibromatosis type 1, sickle cell anemia, and Huntington's disease.

Recently, tests have been developed to detect mutations for a handful of more complex conditions such as breast, ovarian, and colon cancers. Although they have limitations, these tests sometimes are used to make risk estimates in pre-symptomatic individuals with a family history of the disorder.

One potential benefit to using these gene tests is that they could provide information that helps physicians and patients manage the disease or condition more effectively. Regular colonoscopies for those having mutations associated with colon cancer, for instance, could prevent thousands of deaths each year.

Some scientific limitations are that the tests may not detect every mutation associated with a particular condition (many are as yet undiscovered), and the ones they do detect may present different risks to different people and populations. Another important consideration in gene testing is the lack of effective treatments or preventive measures for many diseases and conditions now being diagnosed or predicted.

Revealing information about risk of future disease can have significant emotional and psychological effects as well. Moreover, the absence of privacy and legal protections can lead to discrimination in employment or insurance or other misuse of personal genetic information. Additionally, because genetic tests reveal information about individuals and their families, test results can affect family dynamics. Results also can pose risks for population groups if they lead to group stigmatization.

Other issues related to gene tests include their effective introduction into clinical practice, the regulation of laboratory quality assurance, the availability of testing for rare diseases, and the education of healthcare providers and patients about correct interpretation and attendant risks.

Pharmacogenomics: Moving Away from "One-Size-Fits-All" Therapeutics

Within the next decade, researchers will begin to correlate DNA variants with individual responses to medical treatments, identify particular subgroups of patients, and develop drugs customized for those populations. The discipline that blends pharmacology with genomic capabilities is called pharmacogenomics.

More than 100,000 people die each year from adverse responses to medications that are beneficial to others. Another 2.2 million experience serious reactions, while others fail to respond at all. DNA variants in genes involved in drug metabolism, particularly the cytochrome P450 multigene family, are the focus of much current research in this area.

Enzymes encoded by these genes are responsible for metabolizing most drugs used today, including many for treating psychiatric, neurological, and cardiovascular diseases. Enzyme function affects patients' responses to both the drug and the dose. Future advances will enable rapid testing to determine the patient's genotype and drastically reduce hospitalization resulting from adverse reactions.

Genomic data and technologies also are expected to make drug development faster, cheaper, and more effective. Most drugs today are based on about 500 molecular targets; genomic knowledge of the genes involved in diseases, disease pathways, and drug-response sites will lead to the discovery of thousands of new targets.

New drugs, aimed at specific sites in the body and at particular biochemical events leading to disease, probably will cause fewer side effects than many current medicines. Ideally, the new genomic drugs could be given earlier in the disease process. As knowledge becomes available to select patients most likely to benefit from a potential drug, pharmacogenomics will speed the design of clinical trials to bring the drugs to market sooner.

Gene Therapy, Enhancement

The potential for using genes themselves to treat disease or enhance particular traits has captured the imagination of the public and the biomedical community. This largely experimental field—gene transfer or gene therapy—holds potential for treating or even curing such genetic and acquired diseases as cancers and AIDS by using normal genes to supplement or replace defective genes or bolster a normal function such as immunity.

More than 500 clinical gene-therapy trials involving about 3500 patients have been identified worldwide (June 2001). The vast majority (78%) take place in the United States, followed by Europe (18%). Although most trials focus on various types of cancer, studies also involve other multigenic and monogenic, infectious, and vascular diseases. Protocols generally are aimed at establishing the safety of gene-delivery procedures rather than effectiveness, and no cures as yet can be attributed to these trials.

Gene transfer still faces many scientific obstacles before it can become a practical approach for treating disease. According to the American Society of Human Genetics' Statement on Gene Therapy, effective progress will be achieved only through continued rigorous research on the most fundamental mechanisms underlying gene delivery and gene expression in animals.

*   *   *

Societal Concerns Arising from the New Genetics

Genomics and Its Impact on Medicine and Society: A 2001 Primer

Since its inception, the Human Genome Project has dedicated funds toward studying the ethical, legal, and social issues surrounding the availability of the new data and capabilities. Examples of such issues follow.

- **Privacy and confidentiality of genetic information.** *Who owns and controls genetic information? Is genetic privacy different from medical privacy?*
- **Fairness in the use of genetic information by insurers, employers, courts, schools, adoption agencies, and the military, among others.** *Who should have access to personal genetic information, and how will it be used?*
- **Psychological impact, stigmatization, and discrimination due to an individual's genetic differences.** *How does personal genetic information affect self-identity and society's perceptions?*
- **Reproductive issues including adequate and informed consent and the use of genetic information in reproductive decision making.** *Do healthcare personnel properly counsel parents about risks and limitations? What are the larger societal issues raised by new reproductive technologies?*
- **Clinical issues including the education of doctors and other health-service providers, people identified with genetic conditions, and the general public; and the implementation of standards and quality-control measures.** *How should health professionals be*

prepared for the new genetics? How can the public be educated to make informed choices? How will genetic tests be evaluated and regulated for accuracy, reliability, and usefulness? (Currently, there is little regulation at the federal level.) *How does society balance current scientific limitations and social risk with long-term benefits?*
- **Fairness in access to advanced genomic technologies.** *Who will benefit? Will there be major worldwide inequities?*
- **Uncertainties associated with gene tests for susceptibilities and complex conditions (e.g., heart disease, diabetes, and Alzheimer's disease).** *Should testing be performed when no treatment is available or when interpretation is unsure? Should children be tested for susceptibility to adult-onset diseases?*
- **Conceptual and philosophical implications regarding human responsibility, free will vs. genetic determinism, and concepts of health and disease.** *Do our genes influence our behavior, and can we control it? What is considered acceptable diversity? Where is the line drawn between medical treatment and enhancement?*
- **Health and environmental issues concerning genetically modified (GM) foods and microbes.** *Are GM foods and other products safe for humans and the environment? How will these technologies affect developing nations' dependence on industrialized nations?*

Commercialization of products including property rights (patents, copyrights, and trade secrets) and accessibility of data and materials. *Will patenting DNA sequences limit their accessibility and development into useful products?*

*   *   *

Chapter Nine

How to Interview Older Adults for Intergenerational Writing about their Genealogy and Memories

Working with Intergenerational Writing or Older Writers

STEP 1: Send students in any grade from age 9 to 17 to senior community centers, nursing homes, or senior apartment complexes activity rooms.

STEP 2: Have each student bring a tape recorder with tape and a note pad.

STEP 3: Assign each student one or two older persons to interview with the following questions.
1. What were the most significant turning points or events in your life?
2. How did you survive the Wars?
3. What were the highlights, turning points, or significant events that you experienced during the economic downturn of 1929-1939? How did you cope or solve your problems?

4. What did you do to solve your problems during the significant stages of your life at age 10, 20, 30, 40, 50, 60 and 70-plus? Or pick a year that you want to talk about.

5. What changes in your life do you want to remember and pass on to future generations?

6. What was the highlight of your life?

7. How is it best to live your life after 70?

8. What years do you remember most?

9. What was your favorite stage of life?

10. What would you like people to remember about you and the times you lived through?

STEP 3:

Have the student record the older person's answers. Select the most significant events, experiences, or turning points the person chooses to emphasize. Write the story of that significant event in ten pages or less.

STEP 4: Ask the older person to supply the younger student photos, art work, audio tapes, or video clips. Usually photos, pressed flowers, or art work will be supplied. Have the student or teacher scan the photos onto a disk and return the original photos or
art work or music to the owner.

STEP 5: The student and/or teacher scans the photos and puts them onto a Web site on the Internet at one of the free communities that give away Web site to the public at no cost....some include http://www.tripod.com, http://www.fortunecity.com, http://www.angelfire.com , http://www.geocities.com , and others. Most search engines will give a list of communities at offering free Web sites to the public. Microsoft also offers free family Web sites for family photos and newsletters or information. Ask your Internet service provider whether it offers free Web site space to subscribers.

1. Create a Web site with text from the older person's significant life events
2. Add photos.
3. Add sound or .wav files with the voice of the older person speaking in small clips or sound bites.
4. Intersperse text and photos or art work with sound, if available.
Add video clips, if available and won't take too much bandwidth.
5. Put Web site on line as TIME CAPSULE of (insert name of person) interviewed and edited by, insert name of student who interviewed older person.

STEP 6: Label each Web site Time Capsule and collect them in a history archives on the lives of older adults at the turn of the millennium. Make sure the older person and all relatives and friends are emailed the Web site link. You have now created a time capsule for future generations.

This can be used as a classroom exercise in elementary and high schools to teach the following:

1. Making friends with older adults.
2. Learning to write on intergenerational topics.
3. Bringing community together of all generations.
4. Learning about foster grandparents.
5. History lessons from those who lived through history.
6. Learning about diversity and how people of diverse origins lived through the 20th century.

7. Preserving the significant events in the lives of people as time capsules for future generations to know what it was like to live between 1900 and 2000 at any age.
8. Learning to write skits and plays from the life stories of older adults taken down by young students.
9. Teaching older adults skills in creative writing at senior centers.
10. Learning what grandma did during World War 2 or the stock market crash of 1929 followed by the economic downturn of 1930-1938.

What to Ask People about Their Lives

Step 1
When you interview, ask for facts and concrete details. Look for statistics, and research whether statistics are deceptive in your case.

Step 2
To write a plan, write one sentence for each topic that moves the story or piece forward. Then summarize for each topic in a paragraph. Use dialogue at least in every third paragraph.

Step 3

Look for the following facts or headings to organize your plan for a biography or life story.

1. SLOGAN. Ask the people you interview what would be their slogan if they had to create/invent a slogan that fit themselves or their aspirations: One slogan might be something like the seventies ad for ciga-

rettes, "We've come a long way, baby," to signify ambition. Only look for an original slogan.

2. CRUSADE. Ask the people you interview or a biography, for what purpose is or was their crusade? Is or was it equality in the workplace or something personal and different such as dealing with change—downsizing, working after retirement, or anything else?

3. IMPACT. Ask what makes an impact on people's lives and what impact the people you're interviewing want to make on others?

4. STATISTICS: How deceptive are they? How can you use them to focus on reality?

5. How have the people that you're interviewing influenced changes in the way people or corporations function?

6. To what is the person aspiring?

7. What kind of communication skills does the person have and how are these skills received? Are the communication skills male or female, thinking or feeling, yin or yang, soft or steeled, and are people around these people negative or positive about those communication skills?

8. What new styles is the person using? What kind of motivational methods, structure, or leadership? Is the person a follower or leader? How does the person match his or her personality to the character of a corporation or interest?

9. How does the person handle change?

10. How is the person reinforced?

Once you have titles and summarized paragraphs for each segment of your story, you can more easily flesh out the story by adding dialogue and description to your factual information. Look for differences in style between the people you interview? How does the person want to be remembered?

Is the person a risk taker or cautious for survival? Does the person identify with her job or the people involved in the process of doing the work most creatively or originally? Does creative expression take precedence over processes of getting work out to the right place at the right time? Does the person want his ashes to spell the word "love" where the sea meets the shore?

Search the Records in the Family History Library of Salt Lake City, Utah

Make use of the database online at the Family History Library of Salt Lake City, Utah. Or visit the branches in many locations. The Family History Library (FHL) is known worldwide as the focal point of family history records preservation.

The FHL collection contains more than 2.2 million rolls of microfilmed genealogical records, 742,000 microfiche, 300,000 books, and 4,500 periodicals that represent data collected from over 105 countries. You don't have to be a member of any particular church or faith to use the library or to go online and search the records.

Family history records owe a lot to the invention of writing. And then there is oral history, but someone needs to transcribe oral history to record and archive them for the future.

Interestingly, isn't it a coincidence that writing is 6,000 years old and DNA that existed 6,000 years ago first reached such crowded conditions in the very cities that had first used writing extensively to measure accounting and trade had very little recourse but to move on to new areas where there were far less people and less use of writing?

A lot of major turning points occurred 6,000 years ago—the switch to a grain-based diet from a meat and root diet, the use of bread and fermented grain beverages, making of oil from plants, and the rise of religions based on building "god houses" in the centers of town in areas known as the "cereal belt" around the world.

Six thousand years ago in India we have the start of the Sanskrit writings, the cultivation of grain. In China, we have the recording of acupuncture points for medicine built on energy meridians that also show up in the blue tattoos of the 5,000-year-old Ice Man fossil called "Otsi" found frozen in the Alps—along the same meridians as the Chinese acupuncture points.

At 6,000 years ago the Indo European languages spread out across Europe. Mass migrations expanded by the Danube leaving pottery along the trade routes that correspond to the clines and gradients of gene frequency coming out of the cereal belts.

Then something happened. There was an agricultural frontier cutting off the agriculturists from the hunters. Isn't it a coincidence that the ancient agricultural frontiers or barriers also are genetic barriers at least to some degree?

*   *   *

Oral History

Here's how to systematically collect, record, and preserve living peoples' testimonies about their own experiences. After you record in audio and/or video the highlights of anyone's experiences, try to verify your findings. See whether you can check any facts in order to find out whether the person being recorded is making up the story or whether it really did happen.

This is going to be difficult unless you have witnesses or other historical records. Once you have verified your findings to the best of your ability, note whether the findings have been verified. Then analyze what you found. Put the oral history recordings in an accurate historical context.

Mark the recordings with the dates and places. Watch where you store your findings so scholars in the future will be able to access the transcript or recording and convert the recording to another, newer technology. For instance, if you have a transcript on paper, have it saved digitally on a disk and somewhere else on tape and perhaps a written transcript on acid-free good paper in case technology moves ahead before the transcript or recording is converted to the new technology.

For example, if you only put your recording on a phonograph record, within a generation or two, there may not be any phonographs around to play the record. The same goes for CDs, DVDs and audio or video tapes.

So make sure you have a readable paper copy to be transcribed or scanned into the new technology as well as the recordings on disk and tape. For example, if you record someone's experiences in a live interview with your video camera, use a cable to save the video in the hard disk of a computer and then burn the file to a CD or DVD. Keep a copy of audio tape and a copy of regular video tape—all in a safe place such as a time capsule, and make a copy for various archives in libraries and university oral history preservation centers. Be sure scholars in the future can find a way to enjoy the experiences in your time capsule, scrapbook, or other storage device for oral histories.

Use your DNA testing results to add more information to a historical record. As an interviewer with a video camera and/or audio tape recorder, your task is to record as a historical record what the person who you are interviewing recollects.

The events move from the person being interviewed to you, the interviewer, and then into various historical records. In this way you can combine results of DNA testing with actual memories of events. If it's possible, also take notes or have someone take notes in case the tape doesn't pick up sounds clearly.

I had the experience of having a video camera battery go out in spite of all precautions when I was interviewing someone, and only the audio worked. So keep a backup battery on hand whether you use a tape recorder or a video camera. If at all possible, have a partner bring a spare camera and newly recharged battery. A fully charged battery left overnight has a good chance of going out when you need it.

What Should Go Into an Oral History?

Emphasize the commitment to family and faith. To create readers' and media attention to an oral history, it should have some redemptive value to a universal audience. That's the most important point. Make your oral history simple and earthy. Write about real people who have values, morals, and a faith in something greater than themselves that is equally valuable to readers or viewers.

Publishers who buy an oral history written as a book on its buzz value are buying simplicity. It is simplicity that sells and nothing else but simplicity. This is true for oral histories, instructional materials, and fiction. It's good storytelling to say it simply.

Simplicity means the oral history or memoirs book or story gives you all the answers you were looking for in your life in exotic places, but found it close by. What's the great proverb that your oral history is telling the world?

Is it to stand on your own two feet and put bread on your own table for your family? That's the moral point, to pull your own weight, and pulling your own weight is a buzz word that sells oral histories and fiction that won't preach, but instead teach and reach through simplicity.

That's the backbone of the oral historian's new media. Buzz means the story is simple to understand. You make the complex easier to grasp. And buzz means you can sell your story or book, script or narrative by focusing on the values of simplicity, morals, faith, and universal values that hold true for everyone. Doing the best to take care of your family sells and is buzz appeal, hot stuff in the publishing market of today and in the oral history archives. This is true, regardless of genre. Publishers go through fads every two years—angel books, managing techniques books, computer home-based business books, novels about ancient historical characters or tribes, science fiction, children's programming, biography, and oral history transcribed into a book or play.

The genres shift emphasis, but values are consistent in the bestselling books. Perhaps your oral history will be simple enough to become a bestselling book or script. In the new media, simplicity is buzz along with values. Oral history, like best-selling novels and true stories is built on simplicity, values, morals, and commitment. Include how one person dealt with about trends. Focus your own oral history about life in the lane of your choice.

Steps to Take in Gathering Oral Histories

Use the following sequence when gathering oral/aural histories:

1. Develop one central issue and divide that issue into a few important questions that highlight or focus on that one central issue.
2. Write out a plan just like a business plan for your oral history project. You may have to use that plan later to ask for a grant for

funding, if required. Make a list of all your products that will result from the oral history when it's done.
3. Write out a plan for publicity or public relations and media relations. How are you going to get the message to the public or special audiences?
4. Develop a budget. This is important if you want a grant or to see how much you'll have to spend on creating an oral history project.
5. List the cost of video taping and editing, packaging, publicity, and help with audio or special effects and stock shot photos of required.
6. What kind of equipment will you need? List that and the time slots you give to each part of the project. How much time is available? What are your deadlines?
7. What's your plan for a research? How are you going to approach the people to get the interviews? What questions will you ask?
8. Do the interviews. Arrive prepared with a list of questions. It's okay to ask the people the kind of questions they would like to be asked. Know what dates the interviews will cover in terms of time. Are you covering the economic depression of the thirties? World Wars? Fifties? Sixties? Pick the time parameters.
9. Edit the interviews so you get the highlights of experiences and events, the important parts. Make sure what's important to you also is important to the person you interviewed.
10. Find out what the interviewee wants to emphasize perhaps to highlight events in a life story. Create a video-biography of the highlights of one person's life or an oral history of an event or series of events.
11. Process audio as well as video, and make sure you have written transcripts of anything on audio and/or video in case the technology changes or the tapes go bad.
12. Save the tapes to compact disks, DVDs, a computer hard disk and several other ways to preserve your oral history time capsule.

Donate any tapes or CDs to appropriate archives, museums, relatives of the interviewee, and one or more oral history libraries. They are usually found at universities that have an oral history department and library such as UC Berkeley and others.
13. Check the Web for oral history libraries at universities in various states and abroad.
14. Evaluate what you have edited. Make sure the central issue and central questions have been covered in the interview. Find out whether newspapers or magazines want summarized transcripts of the audio and/or video with photos.
15. Contact libraries, archives, university oral history departments and relevant associations and various ethnic genealogy societies that focus on the subject matter of your central topic.
16. Keep organizing what you have until you have long and short versions of your oral history for various archives and publications. Contact magazines and newspapers to see whether editors would assign reporters to do a story on the oral history project.
17. Create a scrapbook with photos and summarized oral histories. Write a synopsis of each oral history on a central topic or issue. Have speakers give public presentations of what you have for each person interviewed and/or for the entire project using highlights of several interviews with the media for publicity. Be sure your project is archived properly and stored in a place devoted to oral history archives and available to researchers and authors.

Aural History Techniques

1. Begin with easy to answer questions that don't require you explore and probe deeply in your first question. Focus on one central issue when asking questions.

2. First research written or visual resources before you begin to seek an oral history of a central issue, experience, or event.
3. Who is your intended audience?
4. What kind of population niche or sample will you target?
5. What means will you select to choose who you will interview? What group of people will be central to your interview?
6. Write down how you'll explain your project. Have a script ready so you don't digress or forget what to say on your feet.
7. Consult oral history professionals if you need more information. Make sure what you write in your script will be clear to understand by your intended audience.
8. Have all the equipment you need ready and keep a list of what you'll use and the cost. Work up your budget.
9. Choose what kind of recording device is best—video, audio, multimedia, photos, and text transcript. Make sure your video is broadcast quality. I use a Sony Digital eight (high eight) camera.
10. Make sure from cable TV stations or news stations that what type of video and audio you choose ahead of time is broadcast quality.
11. Make sure you have an external microphone and also a second microphone as a second person also tapes the interview in case the quality of your camera breaks down. You can also keep a tape recorder going to capture the audio in case your battery dies.
12. Make sure your battery is fully charged right before the interview. Many batteries die down after a day or two of nonuse.
13. Test all equipment before the interview and before you leave your office or home. I've had batteries go down unexpectedly and happy there was another person ready with another video camera waiting and also an audio tape version going.
14. Make sure the equipment works if it's raining, hot, cold, or other weather variations. Test it before the interview. Practice interviewing someone on your equipment several times to get the hang of it before you show up at the interview.

15. Make up your mind how long the interview will go before a break and use tape of that length, so you have one tape for each segment of the interview. Make several copies of your interview questions.
16. Be sure the interviewee has a copy of the questions long before the interview so the person can practice answering the questions and think of what to say or even take notes. Keep checking your list of what you need to do.
17. Let the interviewee make up his own questions if he wants. Perhaps your questions miss the point. Present your questions first. Then let him embellish the questions or change them as he wants to fit the central issue with his own experiences.
18. Call the person two days and then one day before the interview to make sure the individual will be there on time and understands how to travel to the location. Or if you are going to the person's home, make sure you understand how to get there.
19. Allow yourself one extra hour in case of traffic jams.
20. Choose a quiet place. Turn off cell phones and any ringing noises. Make sure you are away from barking dogs, street noise, and other distractions.
21. Before you interview make sure the person knows he or she is going to be video and audio-taped.
22. If you don't want anyone swearing, make that clear it's for public archives and perhaps broadcast to families.
23. Your interview questions should follow the journalist's information-seeking format of asking, who, what, where, where, how, and why. Oral history is a branch of journalistic research.
24. Let the person talk and don't interrupt. You be the listener and think of oral history as aural history from your perspective.
25. Make sure only one person speaks without being interrupted before someone else takes his turn to speak.
26. Understand silent pauses are for thinking of what to say.

27. Ask one question and let the person gather his thoughts.
28. Finish all your research on one question before jumping to the next question. Keep it organized by not jumping back to the first question after the second is done. Stay in a linear format.
29. Follow up what you can about any one question, finish with it, and move on to the next question without circling back. Focus on listening instead of asking rapid fire questions as they would confuse the speaker.
30. Ask questions that allow the speaker to begin to give a story, anecdote, life experience, or opinion along with facts. Don't ask questions that can be answered only be yes or no. This is not a courtroom. Let the speaker elaborate with facts and feelings or thoughts.
31. Late in the interview, start to ask questions that explore and probe for deeper answers.
32. Wrap up with how the person solved the problem, achieved results, reached a conclusion, or developed an attitude, or found the answer. Keep the wrap-up on a light, uplifting note.
33. Don't leave the individual hanging in emotion after any intensity of. Respect the feelings and opinions of the person. He or she may see the situation from a different point of view than someone else. So respect the person's right to feel as he does. Respect his need to recollect his own experiences.
34. Interview for only one hour at a time. If you have only one chance, interview for an hour. Take a few minutes break. Then interview for the second hour. Don't interview more than two hours at any one meeting.
35. Use prompts such as paintings, photos, music, video, diaries, vintage clothing, crafts, antiques, or memorabilia when appropriate. Carry the photos in labeled files or envelopes to show at appropriate times in order to prime the memory of the interviewee. For example, you may show a childhood photo and ask "What was it

like in that orphanage where these pictures were taken?" Or travel photos might suggest a trip to America as a child, or whatever the photo suggests. For example, "Do you remember when this ice cream parlor inside the ABC movie house stood at the corner of X and Y Street? Did you go there as a teenager? What was your funniest memory of this movie theater or the ice cream store inside back in the fifties?"

36. As soon as the interview is over, label all the tapes and put the numbers in order.
37. A signed release form is required before you can broadcast anything. So have the interviewee sign a release form before the interview.
38. Make sure the interviewee gets a copy of the tape and a transcript of what he or she said on tape. If the person insists on making corrections, send the paper transcript of the tape for correction to the interviewee. Edit the tape as best you can or have it edited professionally.
39. Make sure you comply with all the corrections the interviewee wants changed. He or she may have given inaccurate facts that need to be corrected on the paper transcript.
40. Have the tape edited with the corrections, even if you have to make a tape at the end of the interviewee putting in the corrections that couldn't be edited out or changed.
41. As a last resort, have the interviewee redo the part of the tape that needs correction and have it edited in the tape at the correct place marked on the tape. Keep the paper transcript accurate and up to date, signed with a release form by the interviewee.
42. Oral historians write a journal of field notes about each interview. Make sure these get saved and archived so they can be read with the transcript.
43. Have the field notes go into a computer where someone can read them along with the transcript of the oral history tape or CD.

44. Thank the interviewee in writing for taking the time to do an interview for broadcast and transcript.
45. Put a label on everything you do from the interview to the field notes. Make a file and sub file folders and have everything stored in a computer, in archived storage, and in paper transcript.
46. Make copies and digital copies of all photos and put into the records in a computer. Return originals to owners.
47. Make sure you keep your fingerprints off the photos by wearing white cotton gloves. Use cardboard when sending the photos back and pack securely. Also photocopy the photos and scan the photos into your computer. Treat photos as antique art history in preservation.
48. Make copies for yourself of all photos, tapes, and transcripts. Use your duplicates, and store the original as the master tape in a place that won't be used often, such as a time capsule or safe, or return to a library or museum where the original belongs.
49. Return all original photos to the owners. An oral history archive library or museum also is suitable for original tapes. Use copies only to work from, copy, or distribute.
50. Index your tapes and transcripts. To use oral history library and museum terminology, recordings and transcripts are given "accession numbers."
51. Phone a librarian in an oral history library of a university for directions on how to assign accession numbers to your tapes and transcripts if the materials are going to be stored at that particular library. Store copies in separate places in case of loss or damage.
52. If you don't know where the materials will be stored, use generic accession numbers to label your tapes and transcripts. Always keep copies available for yourself in case you have to duplicate the tapes to send to an institution, museum, or library, or to a broadcast company.

53. Make synopses available to public broadcasting radio and TV stations.
54. Check your facts.
55. Are you missing anything you want to include?
56. Is there some place you want to send these tapes and transcripts such as an ethnic museum, radio show, or TV satellite station specializing in the topics on the tapes, such as public TV stations? Would it be suitable for a world music station? A documentary station?
57. If you need more interviews, arrange them if possible.
58. Give the interviewee a copy of the finished product with the corrections. Make sure the interviewee signs a release form that he or she is satisfied with the corrections and is releasing the tape to you and your project.
59. Store the tapes and transcripts in a library or museum or at a university or other public place where it will be maintained and preserved for many generations and restored when necessary.
60. You can also send copies to a film repository or film library that takes video tapes, an archive for radio or audio tapes for radio broadcast or cable TV.
61. Copies may be sent to various archives for storage that lasts for many generations. Always ask whether there are facilities for restoring the tape. A museum would most likely have these provisions as would a large library that has an oral history library project or section.
62. Make sure the master copy is well protected and set up for long-term storage in a place where it will be protected and preserved.
63. If the oral history is about events in history, various network news TV stations might be interested. Film stock companies may be interested in copies of old photos.

64. Find out from the subject matter what type of archives, repository, or storage museums and libraries would be interested in receiving copies of the oral history tapes and transcripts.
65. Print media libraries would be interested in the hard paper copy transcripts and photos as would various ethnic associations and historical preservation societies. Find out whether the materials will go to microfiche, film, or be digitized and put on CDs and DVDs, or on the World Wide Web. If you want to create a time capsule for the Web, you can ask the interviewee whether he or she wants the materials or selected materials to be put online or on CD as multimedia or other. Then you would get a signed release from the interviewee authorizing you to put the materials or excerpts online. Also find out in whose name the materials are copyrighted and whether you have print and electronic rights to the material or do the owners-authors-interviewees—or you, the videographer-producer? Get it all in writing, signed by those who have given you any interviews, even if you have to call your local intellectual property rights attorney.

How Accurate Are Oral/Aural Histories?

Cameras give fragments, points of view, and bits and pieces. Viewers will see what the videographer or photographer intends to be seen. The interviewee will also be trying to put his point of view across and tell the story from his perspective. Will the photographer or videographer be in agreement with the interviewee? Or if you are recording for print transcript, will your point of view agree with the interviewee's perspective and experience if your basic 'premise,' where you two are coming from, are not in agreement? Think this over as you write your list of questions. Do both of you agree on your central issue on which you'll focus for the interview?

How are you going to turn spoken words into text for your paper hard copy transcript? Will you transcribe verbatim, correct the grammar, or quote as you hear the spoken words? Oral historians really need to transcribe the exact spoken word. You can leave out the 'ahs' and 'oms' or loud pauses, as the interviewee thinks what to say next. You don't want to sound like a court reporter, but you do want to have an accurate record transcribed of what was spoken.

You're also not editing for a movie, unless you have permission to turn the oral history into a TV broadcast, where a lot gets cut out of the interview for time constraints. For that, you'd need written permission so words won't be taken out of context and strung together in the editing room to say something different from what the interviewee intended to say.

Someone talking could put in wrong names, forget what they wanted to say, or repeat themselves. They could mumble, ramble, or do almost anything. So you would have to sit down and weed out redundancy when you can or decide on presenting exactly what you've heard as transcript. When someone reads the transcript in text, they won't have what you had in front of you, and they didn't see and hear the live presentation or the videotape. It's possible to misinterpret gestures or how something is spoken, the mood or tone, when reading a text transcript. Examine all your sources. Use an ice-breaker to get someone talking.

If a woman is talking about female-interest issues, she may feel more comfortable talking to another woman. Find out whether the interviewee is more comfortable speaking to someone of his or her own age. Some older persons feel they can relate better to someone close to their own age than someone in high school, but it varies. Sometimes older people can speak more freely to a teenager.

The interviewee must be able to feel comfortable with the interviewer and know he or she will not be judged. Sometimes it helps if the interviewer is the same ethnic group or there is someone present of the same group or if new to the language, a translator is present.

Read some books on oral history field techniques. Read the National Genealogical Society Quarterly (NGSQ). Also look at The American Genealogist (TAG), The Genealogist, and The New England Historical and Genealogical Register (The Register). If you don't know the maiden name of say, your grandmother's mother, and no relative knows either because it wasn't on her death certificate, try to reconstruct the lives of the males who had ever met the woman whose maiden name is unknown.

Maybe she did business with someone before marriage or went to school or court. Someone may have recorded the person's maiden name before her marriage. Try medical records if any were kept. There was no way to find my mother's grandmother's maiden name until I started searching to see whether she had any brothers in this country. She had to have come as a passenger on a ship around 1880 as she bought a farm. Did her husband come with her?

Was the farm in his name? How many brothers did she have in this country with her maiden surname? If the brothers were not in this country, what countries did they come from and what cities did they live in before they bought the farm in Albany? If I could find out what my great grandmother's maiden name was through any brothers living at the time, I could contact their descendants perhaps and see whether any male or female lines are still in this country or where else on the globe.

Perhaps a list of midwives in the village at the time is recorded in a church or training school for midwives. Fix the person in time and place. Find out whom she might have done business with and whether any records of that business exist. What businesses did she patronize? Look for divorce or court records, change of name records, and other legal documents.

Look at local sources. Did anyone save records from bills of sale for weddings, purchases of homes, furniture, debutante parties, infant supplies, or even medical records? Look at nurses' licenses, midwives' registers, employment contracts, and teachers' contracts, alumni associations for various schools, passports, passenger lists, alien registration cards, naturalization records, immigrant aid societies, city directories, and cross-references.

Try religious and women's clubs, lineage and village societies, girl scouts and similar groups, orphanages, sanatoriums, hospitals, police records. Years ago there was even a Eugenics Record Office. What about the women's prisons? The first one opened in 1839—Mount Pleasant Female Prison, NY.

Try voters' lists. If your relative is from another country, try records in those villages or cities abroad. Who kept the person's diaries? Have you checked the Orphan Train records? Try ethnic and religious societies and genealogy associations for that country. Most ethnic genealogy societies have a special interest group for even the smallest villages in various countries.

You can start one and put up a Web site for people who also come from there in past centuries. Check alimony, divorce, and court records, widow's pensions of veterans, adoptions, orphanages, foster homes, medical records, birth, marriage, and death certificates, social security, immigration, pet license owners' files, prisons, alumni groups from schools, passenger lists, military, and other legal records.

When all historical records are being tied together, you can add the DNA testing to link all those cousins. Check military pensions on microfilms in the National Archives. See the bibliography section of this book for further resources on highly recommended books and articles on oral history field techniques and similar historical subjects.

* * *

Does Writing Your Life Story As A Genealogy and/or Novel Affect Your Memory?

Oral history depends on memory and the ability to speak. I also think of oral history as aural history, based on the ability to hear someone's experiences and remember them to pass on to the next generation or the world.

To find out the effects of oral history on memory and on creative writing on memory, we'd have to ask the people who write their life story and/or genealogy in their older years what it did for them, their memory, and their ability to think and feel. Make use of introverted feeling in writing a commercial or salable life story for the new media. Think in three dimensions for older adults is a different highway. How did DNA testing influence a genealogy search for family history facts?

Did the individual create a time capsule? How was the time capsule saved—on the Web? On a CD, DVD, video, or audio tape? In a scrapbook of photos, with various memorabilia? Did anyone rescue old photos from antique stores and flea markets by searching for photographer's prints on the front or back of the photo or names on the back of the photo and dates or locations?

1. When turning your salable life story, corporate history, or biography into an adventure action romance novel, don't set up your main characters in the first chapter to be in transit traveling on board a plane, train, or ship going somewhere. The action actually starts or hits them after they have already arrived at their destination.

Start your first chapter when your characters already get to their destination place or point in time. A first chapter that opens when your main character is on a plane or train is the kiss of death from many editors point of view and the main reason why a good novel often is rejected. So cut out the traveling scene from your first chapter and begin where the action starts for real, at the destination point. Does anyone visit antique stores, malls, or flea markets to search for family history memorabilia? What about attic, basement, or garage sales?

2. Use a lot of dialogue when turning a biography or your life story into a salable novel, especially in a romance, adventure action, or suspense novel or in one where you combine romance with adventure and suspense.

Use no more than three pages of narrative without dialogue. Let characters speak through the dialogue and tell the reader what is happening. Get characters to speak as normally as possible. If the times and place dictate they speak in proverbs, so be it. Proverbs make the best novels as you turn your proverb into a story and play it out as a novel. Otherwise, have normal speech so you can be the catalyst and bring people together who understand clearly what one another means.

3. Put your characters on the stage and have them talking to one another. If you have introspection in your book, don't use introspection for your action line. Action adventure books keep characters on stage talking to the audience.

4. Use magazines and clothing catalogues to make a collage of what your character might look like. This inspiration may go up on a board in front of you or on the wall to see as you work. Get a picture in your mind of what your characters look like. If they don't exist in art history, draw them yourself or make a mixed media collage of what they look like, speak like, and stand for. Some ideas include the models in "cigar" magazines, catalogues, and fashion publications as well as multi-ethnic and historical illustrations and photos.

5. Research history and keep a loose-leaf notebook with tabs on the history of places you want to research. The history itself is great for ideas on what plot to write. Look at or visit old forts and similar places. Plug in characters to your research. Look at forts of foreign settlements in the country of your choice, U.S. or any other place. Record the dates in your files. Create a spreadsheet in Excel or any other type of spread sheet with your dates from historical research as these will relate to your characters and help you develop a real plot.

6. Keep a notebook for each novel or biography you write. Put everything related to each book in a notebook. Have one notebook for historical research and one for the novel you're writing or true storybook.

7. When sending out your book manuscript make a media kit for yourself with your resume, photo, list of works in development if you are not yet published, and any other material about your own experience in any other field.

8. Your own biography and photo presented to the press also can be used to let an editor know when you send out your manuscript of what's in development and what you've done. It's not necessary to continue ethnic stereotypes in your book. If one of your characters is a music agent, for example, and a lot of music agents are of one ethnicity or speak with a certain accent, it's not necessary to continue the stereotyping roles. Pick something new for a change. Otherwise it becomes cliché. Research as many diverse ways of telling the same story as you can.

9. Write down the point of view before your book is begun. Whose point of view is it anyway? Who tells the story?

10. If you're writing a romance novel from your life story or a military romantic suspense novel, true story, radio script, or other genre, agree on the point of view before you start. Who's telling the story and how does she or he know how the other characters know what to say?

11. The readers needs to learn facts or experiences, anecdotes, oral histories transcribed, and stories that have not been generalized. Use a series of incidents, action and relationship tension to balance your plot with your dialogue.

12. If you're turning a biography into a romance novel, you need to balance the relationship tension with the mystery, action, or other plot. You must have some event occur on both sides, on the sexual tension side and on the mystery or action side to balance out the book.

13. For every action in a life story, there's an equal and opposite reaction that's primarily character-driven and secondarily plot-driven. And in an autobiography or anyone's life story, relationship tension occurs. Then the plot moves on. If it's a romantic suspense or mystery within a life story, such as true confession, true crime, or biography, usually twenty-four short chapters makes a book-length story.

14. A diary is written in first person as a journal or log, but a biography can be of you or your client. Even in a memoirs book or diary, you have to balance action with interaction between the heroine and the hero.

15. You can be the only person in your diary, but the action and interaction needs to be balanced with something out there in the external world—either forces of nature or another person—or the competition.

16. If you keep the competition out of your diary, put in the memories, actions, and warmth of the friends, including pets. If there are no other people, put in some force of spirit, some other push and pull, or tension, for balance with something outside yourself. This can be a job, school, a hobby, or what you choose as the force that pulls in an opposite direction existing with the force or person that pulls in your direction.

17. Try putting the relationship tension between the hero and heroine in the even-numbered chapters, and the mystery, historical events, or action plot events in the odd-numbered chapters.

18. In a 24-chapter- historical romance, this alternating action chapter, romantic tension chapter balances the plot smoothly. Most historical romance novels have 22-24 chapters. If you analyze the best-selling ones, you'll see that chapter one has an opening scene on the action side so you see what's happening.

19. The first action-oriented introductory chapter that shows us what's happening is followed by the second chapter on the romantic tension side showing us when and how the heroine meets the hero or has a re-union with the hero.

20. In the second chapter, the writer takes the heroine somewhere in place or time. The heroine in the second chapter is defined. Either she's a 90's woman, or she's in her place in history or rebelling against it. You tell the story. If you're male, you'd use a hero.

21. True life stories featuring genealogy combined with biography usually are 10-12 chapters long. Historical romances are twice that size at 22-24 chapters. The writer decides whether it's best to turn a biography into a historical romance or a life story into a mystery, suspense, action adventure, young adult novel, romance, or other genre.

22. If you are not fictionalizing genealogy or biography into a story, keep your time capsule book, database, or other media true to facts and historical records only. You might want to add your DNA testing records of relatives along with a family tree or other database or time capsule.

23. For those who want to turn factual biography into a novel, in turning a biography into a romance, the romantic tension side is about girl meeting hero in the first chapter.

24. In the second chapter, the hero takes her somewhere in place, space, time, or state of mind. An oral history may be written as true life story in the form of a novel or play, skit, or anecdote of experience.

25. Oral histories highlight a life experience within a time frame set in one or more locations with all the nuances of that place. It's basically

a life story, but it can be transcribed with that certain something, including—charisma, liveliness, action, forward movement, drama, tension, and unique experiences, problems solved, and goals.

* * *

CHAPTER TEN

Diaries Plus DNA

What do diaries and DNA tests have in common? Both are handled as evidence.

Diaries, like deleted files hidden in the cache pits of computers, and DNA tests can be used as evidence. Diaries also hold the seeds of a story. You could write a novel or a screenplay from a diary. A diary also is a history. So preserve a diary as you would restore and preserve a valuable work of art from the past. Diaries are meant to be passed to future generations for a glimpse into a world that can be experienced by generations far into the future. Keep a file of dates listed in the diary and any objects that surrounded the diary from the same era.

A story with a central issue needed little explanation when my mom wrote in her diary in the style of a telegram: "October 25, 1926: First day of honeymoon. On train to Miami. Today I died." What central issues and themes tell a story in the diaries that cross your path?

Keep the dates and topics organized if you are working with restoring and preserving diaries. There should be a central issue or theme. How old was the person writing the diary? How many years did the individual keep the diary? What kind of objects were near the diary, packed together?

What kind of dust or other stains were on the diary—sawdust? Farm materials and plants? The first corsage from the senior prom? How about recipes, household hints, or how-to tips for hobbies? Was the diary or journal personal and inner-reflected, or geared toward outer events in the world? Were anecdotes about people and/or pets included, or was it about the feelings of the author of the diary?

Find out what other clues the mystery of the diary unfolds, from the lipstick or nail polish stain to the sawdust and coffee stains, or that faint smell of tobacco, industrial lint, or is it lavender, jasmine or farm dust and straw? Look inside the box in which the diary was packed. It's all evidence and clues waiting to be examined just like a mystery novel. A diary is a story, and everyone life deserves a novel, story, or biography and eventually, a place in a time capsule.

In logs or diaries, women asked for connections, and men replied, "Give me a break." Diaries were personal journals. Logs contained facts that were meant to be read by others. In times past, women were said to write in diaries, and men wrote in logs.

Women wrote about their goals, reactions, hopes or feelings, and men detailed facts and kept records about their goals, actions and outlined plans. Men planned, and women wrote spontaneously in logs and diaries. Women connected the dots, or brought people and ideas together to create mind maps in diaries. Men linked objects to other objects. Women wrote about what happened on their honeymoon—the silent body language of gestures and postures in conversation. In those days gone by, women may have used diaries as an escape from the hobble skirts and tight corsets where their only private spaces were in their diaries or inside their purses. Men's knees took up wide spaces in cramped quarters, and the written logs reflected the use of much space. The cultural aspect of oral history can open doors to the biology of the genes and vice versa.

How to Restore a Diary, Log, or Bound Personal Journal

Make a book jacket for your diary to preserve and restore it. Use acid-free paper. Call a library or museum and ask for a brand or type of long-lasting acid-free paper and where you can buy some. Put a title and label on the dust jacket with the name of the diary's author and any dates, city, state, or country.

You can also speak to the art history department of most universities and find out what kind of paper is best to use for a book jacket to restore and preserve a diary. Treat it like a work of art. The same can be done for photo scrap books.

If torn, mend the diary. Your goal is to improve its condition. Apply a protective plastic wrapper to your valuable dust jacket. Give the diary a dust jacket in good condition. It should start to look more like a valuable book in good condition. If the diary is dingy and dirty, bleach it white on the edges. Put a plastic cover on the diary. The white pages of a diary without ink can be bleached with regular household bleach, but don't let the vapors of the bleach soak through to reach the ink because it will bleach out the writing.

Repair old diaries and turn them into heirlooms for families and valuable collectibles. The current price for repair of handwritten diaries and books is about $35 and up per book or bound diary, if you like to specialize in mending old dairies and family or personal books for a fee.

Some old diaries contain recipes and also served as personal, handwritten cookbooks containing recipes created by a particular family or family cook. These were valuable books preserved as if they were family scrapbooks, unlike the recipe databases in computers we have today. They are works of art, like an old tapestry embroidered with the story of a family's major turning points and events.

For more repair tips on bound diaries and books, I recommend *How to Wrap a Book*, Fannie Merit Farmer, Boston Cooking School.

How do you repair an old diary to make it more valuable to the heirs? You'll often find a bound diary that's torn in the seams. According to Barbara Gelink, of the Collector's Old Cookbooks Club, San Diego, to repair a book, you take a bottle of Book Saver Glue (or any other book-repairing or wood glue), and spread the glue along the binder.

Run the glue along the seam and edges. Use wax paper to keep the glue from getting where it shouldn't. Put a heavy glass bottle on the inside page to hold it down while the glue dries.

To remove tape, tags, or stains from a glossy cover, use lighter fluid or cleaning fluid (away from sparks, flames, or heat lamps). Dampen a cloth with nail polish remover if lighter fluid is too smelly and flammable for you.

Another way to remove something pasted on a plastic book cover, is to use the finest grade sandpaper. Many books you'll find at goodwill will have adhesive price tags on the book. It's not usual to find diaries, even bound diaries in old book stores, but they show up in garage sales and in some antique stores and flea markets along with old photos.

To bleach the "discarded book stamp" that libraries often use, or any other rubber stamp mark, price, date, or seals on the pages of a book or on the edges, use regular bleach, like Clorox. It turns the rubber stamp mark white. The household bleach also turns the edges and pages of the book white as new.

To preserve a valuable dust jacket, a tattered jacket with tears along the edges needs extra firmness. A protective plastic wrapper can improve the condition of a book if it has a jacket cover.

To look for old diaries, or old family photos, look in garage sales, flea markets, and antique shops. Attend auctions and book fairs. Two recommended auction houses for rare cookbooks include Pacific Book Auction Galleries, 139 Townsend, #305, San Francisco, CA 94107, or Sotheby's, New York, 1334 York Ave., New York, NY 10021. Pacific Book Auction Galleries recently put a large cookbook collection up for an auction.

Hunt for diaries, old photos, and other old clues to family history in thrift shops and antique stores. Some diaries also combine cookbooks with personal histories and transcribed oral histories, but these are very rare. Genealogy also can have a person's collection of favorite recipes or anything else the person collected organized and archived along with family history and genetics records.

If you're into scrap booking with family history, photos, and recipes, for nostalgia, look for cookbooks printed by high school parent-teacher associations. Some old ones may be valuable, but even the one put out by the depression era San Diego High School Parent Teacher Association for the class of 1933-34 is only worth $10.

To find out-of-print and mail-order cookbooks, contact Charlotte F. Safir, 1349 Lexington Ave #9-B, New York, NY 10128-1513. She specializes in hard-to-find cookbooks and children's books. Astor House Books, PO Box 1701 Williamsburg, VA 23187 specializes in cookery and gastronomy. Amber Unicorn Books, specializes in rare cookbooks. They're at 2202 W. Charleston Blvd, #2, Las Vegas, NV 89102 .

Little Treasures (Joyce Klein) Cookery Books has British and American cookbooks and general stock. They're at 7517 W. Madison, Forest Park, IL 60130. Send your wants because they have no catalog.

Cornucopia, run by Carol A. Greenberg, has cooking and food literature and domestic history, household management, herbs and kitchen gardens, hotels and restaurants, etiquette and manners, pastimes and amusements, and needlework old and rare books. They search for out-of-print books, and are interested in material from the 19th century through 1940. Write to: Little Treasures at PO Box 742, Woodbury, NY 11797. Greenberg is always grateful for quotations on old, rare, and unusual materials in fine condition.

The Collector's Old Cookbooks Club has half their members in other states and half in San Diego County. They send a newsletter to each member after the monthly meeting.

You could specialize in being a diary restoration specialist and book finder for genealogy groups. Perhaps you want to deal in collectors' valuable diaries, largely first editions. Mostly diaries are only editions. Some people had them bound like a blank notebook, and wrote in them. So they look like first editions of books.

Are diaries worth as much as rare cookbooks? How much are the thousands of rare cookbooks worth today? A helpful guide is the <u>Price Guide to Cookbooks & Recipe Leaflets</u>, 1990, by Linda J. Dickinson, published by Collector Books, at PO Box 3009, Paducah, KY 42002-3009.

See <u>Bibliography of American Cookery Books</u>, 1742-1860. It's based on Waldo Lincoln's <u>American Cookery Books</u> 1742-1860, by Eleanor Lowenstein. Over 800 books and pamphlets are listed. Order from Oak Knoll Books & Press, 414 Delaware St., Newcastle, Delaware 19720.

Louis & Clark Booksellers specialize in rare and out-of-print cookery, gastronomy, wine and beverages, baking, restaurants, domestic history, etiquette, and travel books. They're at 2402 Van Hise Avenue, Madison, WI 53705.

Cookbooks and diaries are not that much distant from each other, although diaries of a famous person would have monetary value as would old cookbooks that are rare. Think of the events in the life story and history value of what real people's lives were like many decades or centuries ago. Any restored diaries would be valuable to descendants of anyone, and you can't put a price tag on these people's lives as expressed in diaries.

Get acid-free storage envelopes or boxes for diaries. Handle old diaries and books with gloves, and get rid of mildew safely without destroying the pages or fading the ink. It's here that a library can be helpful. Ask questions about storage from historical societies and libraries. Make copies of the diaries. Work with the photocopies when you decipher the writing.

Store old diaries in a dry, cool place where there are no bugs. Lining the storage place with plastic that's sealed will keep out vermin and bugs. Without moisture, you can keep out the mildew and mold. Store duplicates away from originals.

Call archivists and historians in your area and ask for their advice. Was something placed on a certain page, such as a dried rose, letter, or a special book mark? What meaning did it have? Date the diary. List the date it was begun and when it was ended, or look for clues for a time frame. List the geographic location of the events in the diary or the writer.

Of what kind of materials is the diary made? Is it improvised, created at low cost by the author? Or is it fancy and belonging to someone of wealth? What is the layout like? Does it show the education of the writer or anything personal? Was it a masculine almanac or calendar or a feminine expression of memorabilia and sentiment? Or was it written by a man writing poetry or letters and being romantic?

Can you tell the personality traits of the writer of that diary? What was the writing tool, a quill or a pencil? What's the handwriting like? Would a handwriting analyst know what to say about it? Does the handwriting and words express anger, joy, sadness, or what? Is it full of detail, or is the reader given the big picture? Why was the diary written? What is its central message? Do you see patterns, concepts or facts?

Transcribe the diary with your computer. What historical events influenced the writing of the diary? What language is it in or dialect? Study the historical meaning of the diary so you can get to know the writer across the chasms of decades or centuries.

Are there vital records such as deeds to real estate mentioned in the diary? What photographs are in the diary? Any artifacts mentioned or pressed between the pages? See whether you can relate to the diary author and find some type of context of the story from entry to entry. Are there any genealogical records or mention of family names, such as a great, great, great grandmother's maiden name? What about recorded events of inherited diseases or medical histories?

If the grandfather's dad went blind with glaucoma, it's has a genetic element that heirs should know about whether anyone inherited it or not. See what the diary unfolds that can be read as family history, world history, or used in the phenomics mode, to customize treatment or therapy based on genetics.

Treat the diary as a precious work of art, including the photos in there, if any. Don't touch the old right side up photos with bare fingers because the emulsion would quickly come off. Some genealogists specialize in working with old diaries, and novelists or screenwriters would probably be interested in a unique story. Restore a diary, and if a building such as a restaurant wants to hang old photos in the dining hall, let the photos be copies rather than the originals.

If you want to record the memories of relatives or friends, list 100-200 inspiring questions. Give the questions to relatives and friends. Create the questions with the goal of triggering recall of memories and experiences, events, and highlights of their life stories. Give them a diary and make a dust cover that's fancy. Put a plastic cover over the dust jacket.

Use a hardbound book with a question on each page. Or give several pages per question if the person might like to write for personal expression. You could ask the person if he or she wanted more or less pages. About 150 questions or pages are fine to last a lifetime of a minimum of one-page summarized life events or answers to the questions you ask.

The questions should be important to both you and the person who's going to write in the diary or journal. This is one way to create a genealogy diary gift that develops into a biography from a personal journal or diary.

Make sure there's enough pages and room to express what's required. Print the questions large and clear so you can elicit recorded responses to the questions. Leave room to attach photographs on acid-free, archival-quality paper.

If the person really won't write, create a tape recorded or video diary where the person can record his voice on tape, in a computer, or with a video camera on a tripod poised next to a desk to record the person talking without requiring anyone else in the room when recording.

Give the person a remote control device for the video camera to click on and off without walking toward the camera or tape recorder, or computer microphone. If the person will write at all, stick with the personal ambiance of a diary gift that someone can hold in any location or take traveling.

What questions to write? List thought-starters. Write questions about their childhood, values, dreams, and goals. Create a section for recording time as a mother or father, grandparent, how a child's name was chosen, how the marriages were arranged, or what things each child did to make a parent proud.

Put in blank pages and a place for each relative to put in the results of their DNA testing, fingerprints, print of hand or palm, or any other personal information, even medical notes or other memories in the memorabilia. Leave room for children's photos, small drawings, and meaningful relics. Use the kind of binding where someone can add pages.

File and archive the DNA test results, racial percentages tests, along with any other information from memory. Add an oral history, perhaps a pocket for a tape, or room for a transcript of an oral history to be added, such as a loose-leaf binding or similar binding so pages may be added to folders or plastic envelopes holding mementos. Have a space for the first job and for a father's memories.

The genealogy thought-starter questions can come bound in a fancy, hard-bound loose-leaf that will last as pages are added. Or better yet to give each his or her own individual expression without the judgment of another relative, give a separate book to each family member so he or she can keep memories or traditions private until passed to heirs. You might want to create a separate book for each grandparent, parent, and other relative.

*   *   *

CHAPTER ELEVEN

Mapping Your Personal Anthropology with Genetic Genealogy

Source: Facts & Genes"
<http://www.familytreeDNA.com/facts_genes.asp>.
Reprinted with Permission from:
Facts & Genes, from Family Tree DNA
Copyright 2002, Family Tree DNA),
November 21, 2002 Volume 1, Issue 5
====================================

Family Tree DNA enjoys hearing about the results of your DNA testing. One customer wrote: "Just a word of thanks to you for the work you are doing on this project. The information I received today has already helped direct my genealogical work into a more focused and well-researched area, and has saved innumerable hours of work! Thanks for making this testing available, and for providing it in a financially accessible form. It's appreciated!"

Send comments, suggestions, tips, questions, and tell Family Tree DNA about your Surname Project to: editor@familytreedna.com.

Family Tree DNA is pleased to announce that the ANCESTRYbyDNA test is now available. The ANCESTRYbyDNA test was developed by DNAPrint Genomics, Inc., and is available through Family Tree DNA.

The ANCESTRYbyDNA test will measure a person's Personal Anthropology and their corresponding ancestral ethnic proportions. The result of the test is a report showing your percentages of each ethnic ancestry or major human population group. For example, your result could be 18% Native American, 70% European, and 12% African.

Perhaps you have wondered whether you have any Native American ancestry, or maybe you are just curious to find out more about yourself. The ANCESTRYbyDNA test will unlock the secrets to your ancestors contained in your DNA.

The ANCESTRYbyDNA test analyzes your DNA to determine which of the major human populations your ancestors belonged to, and what percentage you have inherited of these groups. These four geographical areas and the corresponding major human population groups are: Native American, East Asian, European, and sub-Saharan African.

This test, developed by DNAPrint Genomics, utilizes SNP's that are diagnostic of a person's continent of origin. SNP's are deep ancestral locations along the human genome, and have a different result when tested with different peoples.

To order the ANCESTRYbyDNA test, click on this link: http://www.familytreedna.com/products.html#dnaprintorder

Surnames

Are you wondering why the XYZ surname project has over 50 participants, and you only have 6 participants so far? Do you look at your Web site and correspondence, and wonder what is their secret to recruiting participants? The answer may be that they have a larger population of their surname from which to recruit participants. Your Surname Project may actually have a higher percentage of the surname participating than the project with over 50 participants.

It is common knowledge that Smith is the most frequent surname in the US. The chart below shows the 10 most frequent surnames in the US in the 1990 census. For each surname, the percentage represents the percentage of persons in the US with this surname, and the Rank is the ranking of the surname with 1 being the most frequent. For example, in the chart below, eight surnames are more frequent than Moore.

Surname	%	Rank
SMITH	1.006	1
JOHNSON	0.810	2
WILLIAMS	0.699	3
JONES	0.621	4
BROWN	0.621	5
DAVIS	0.480	6
MILLER	0.424	7
WILSON	0.339	8
MOORE	0.312	9
TAYLOR	0.311	10

Assume that a person started a Smith Surname project. There are over 2 million Smith's in the US, of which over 1 million would be males. This is quite a few people. If they signed up 50 people, they have only signed up a very small percentage of the Smith surname.

Compare this to the surname Mumma, which is .001 % of the population, and its Rank is 15,109. There is a much smaller pool of Mumma potential participants. If you look at the surname, Norin, its number is so small in the US 1990 census, that it does not even get a result when the 1990 US census Surname Frequency is searched.

You can find out what percentage of the US population holds your surname by going to the US Government census site at: http://www.census.gov/genealogy/www/freqnames.html

The site also covers the methodology that the Census Bureau used to come up with the percentages and rank for the surnames.

The US population on April 1, 2000 was 281,421,906 people. If you would like a rough idea of the males with your surname in the US, first search the site <http://www.census.gov/genealogy/www/freqnames.html> to get the percentage for your surname. Multiply that percentage times the population of the 2000 census. In their rough calculation, they will assume that 50% are males, so now divide by 2. This is an estimate of the number of males with your surname. To estimate the number of adult males, multiply by .7. The formula is:
Percentage * 281,421,906 / 2 * .7=adult males with surname

You can also find out how common your surname is in the UK at the site: http://www.taliesin-arlein.net/names/search.php. There are 269,353 surnames in the UK database, representing 54,412,638 people. This database is provided by the Office of National Statistics of the UK, and gives an actual count of the number of persons for each surname. Their database is an extract of an Office of National Statistics database, and provides a list of surnames in use in England, Wales and the Isle of Mann in September 2002.

The US Census population database and the Office of National Statistics of the UK database used different methodologies to come up with their results. Rare surnames will not get a search result in the US census site, whereas they will in the UK site, even if there are only a few persons with the same surname. Names shared by fewer than five people have been excluded from the UK list.

Now that you have an idea of the size of your potential prospect pool, lets assume that only 1/3 are interested in genealogy, so you now divide by 3. The end result is a very rough approximation of the number of potential participants available. If you are only using the Internet to find your participants, cut this number in half for the US. Other countries have a smaller percentage of persons on the Internet than the US.

As your first step, you have probably posted your project to as many sites and mailing lists that are applicable and allow such postings. You have probably also put up a web site, even if it is only one page. Most likely you have contacted all those persons whom you had contact with in the past regarding genealogy.

Here are some suggestions to consider in order to make more people aware of your project:

1. Consult the Directory of Family Associations. If there is a Family Association for your surname, contact them and offer to write an article for their publication about your project.

2. Register your web site with familysearch.org. Everyone searching on your surname at Familysearch.org will find your web site. You must first register yourself with familysearch.org to be able to submit your website for consideration.

3. Visit your local Family History Center, and offer to show the Genealogy by Genetics video to the staff and patrons. This might not find you any participants, but if every Group Administrator takes an hour to do this, then all the Surname Projects might find participants.

4. Review your web site. It needs to be easy to understand for those not familiar with DNA testing, and clearly present the benefits to the participant. What will they gain from participating? How will it help them in their research? What might the results tell them?

5. Find out if there are any genealogy clubs or organizations in your area, and volunteer to show the video, and answer questions.

DNA testing for genealogy is a new field, and we are all pioneers. Most likely you have learned a lot about the field as a result of your testing. Those of us who have learned about DNA testing and how to interpret the results are aware of the benefits and how the testing can assist us with our genealogy research.

The majority of those interested in Family History research most likely aren't aware of Genetic Genealogy. If you volunteer an hour to help your fellow genealogists understand this new tool, and help more people become knowledgeable, all of us will benefit as we seek participants for our testing. Look for social histories of the ethnic group you're researching.

When you're working with DNA, you can look for historical medical records. Only a few are open to the public. You might try the microfilmed collections at The Family History Library in Salt Lake City, UT, or rent one of the microfilms from any of the worldwide family history centers, usually found in a genealogical library in various cities around the world.

Look at records from the Eugenics Record Office (ERO) that operated from 1910 to 1944. The purpose of that office was to study human genetics in order to reduce inheritable genetic disorders. You can look over the 520 rolls of microfilm. Visit the Family History Library Catalog and look under United States—Medical Records—Eugenics.

Look up the state you want, and look under Medical Records. You might want to read up on the controversial Eugenics movement. Think about how DNA testing today differs in that the test results are used today either to find relatives, ancestors, or tailor individual therapies for individual genetic make-ups—phenomics. How times have changed. Or have they? What do you see in your own DNA and family history research?

The Family History Library in Salt Lake City also has some historical hospital records. One example is the Northwestern Memorial Hospital record, Chicago in the Family History Library, dated 1896-1933. Perhaps one of your relatives is in those files. That's one other way of finding a maiden name from the days when many people were never given a birth certificate because they were born at home and never registered. That's what happened with my mom, born in 1904 at home in NY state.

Understanding your Results: Ethnic Origin

Whether you are just starting a Surname Project, or ordered a test for yourself to learn about DNA testing for genealogy, everyone experiences the situation of receiving the first test result, and what now? You have one test result, and what do you do with a string of 12 or 25 numbers? Can they tell you anything? Where can you find the information you need?

In the situation of the one or first test result, most likely you will not find others to whom you are related. The odds of a random match to some one to whom you are related when you are the first of your surname to test is slim to none. Instead, you might find some clues to your ethnic origin.

To find clues about your ethnic origin, Log into FamilyTreeDna.com, and at your Personal Page click on Recent Ethnic Origins to search this data base. The results show others whom you match, or who are a near match, and their ancestor's ethnic origin.

The information on their ethnic origin is provided by each person tested (testee). The information provided for ethnic origin is only as accurate as the knowledge held by the testee regarding their ancestors. Testees are instructed to answer unknown for ethnic origin when their ancestor's origin is not known, or not certain. Sometimes the origin the testees provided is incorrect.

Incorrect origins provided by testees may lead to search results that do not seem logical. For example: Assume your ancestors are from England, but your search results show the ethnic origin of your matches as England, France, AND one match shows an origin of Native American. Does that mean that your ancestor's relatives may have lived in England and France? Yes. Does it mean that your ancestor was also a Native American? No. It means that a settler in America had a child with a Native American woman, the child was brought up as a Native

American, and that, over time, the family has "forgotten" the European ancestor, and believes their ancestry to be Native American.

During the span of generations people tend to move, as do borders, so nationality or ethnicity becomes subjective. For example, testees may enter Germany for ethnic origin, because the land of their ancestors is in Germany today, but the land had been held by Denmark for many centuries.

Your search should return at least one match, namely yourself. If your results show 3 matches from Ireland and 1 from Scotland, and you have reported to us that your ancestors came from Scotland, then you are the Scotland result. The other 3 matches are either from the Family Tree DNA database or from the databases Family Tree DNA have been supplied by the University of Arizona.

To see how your ethnic origin is recorded in our database, click on the link titled Update Contact Information. You can also update your paternal and maternal ethnic origin on this Update Contact Information page.

Exact matches show people who are the closest to you genetically. The Ethnic origin shows where they have been reported to have lived. Since many persons migrated since the beginning of time, you will typically see matches in more than one country.

For information purposes, the Recent Ethnic Origin search also displays results for those who are not exact matches, but are 'near matches'. A near match is either one step or two steps from your result. An exact match is 12/12 or 25/25. A one step match is 11/12 or 24/25. A two step match is 10/12 or 23/25. The value of the near matches is to see where those who may be related migrated over time.

Other databases available that you can search are:
European: http://ystr.charite.de/index_gr.html
US: http://www.ystr.org/usa/

In some cases you will not find any results. This is because only a very small percentage of the world population has been tested and is in the databases. The Ystr databases, plus the FamilyTreeDNA Recent Ethnic Origin database together hold about 21,000 test results. Every day more results are added, and it is only a matter of time before you will have some matches. Your test with Family Tree DNA includes access to our databases for matching.

If you do not find any results in the two YSTR databases shown above, try entering your result, and then eliminating a marker, and do this until you have a smaller set of markers that results in some matches. This might provide some clues regarding where your markers have occurred geographically.

The value of DNA testing comes from comparing your results to others. If you have started a Surname Project, you will most likely have results from others soon. If you only tested yourself, you may want to consider either using DNA testing to solve one of your Family History questions, or starting a Surname Project.

Haplotypes: Convergence

A Haplotype is the 12 Marker result from testing the Y chromosome. Some Haplotypes are common, with a high frequency of occurrence and some Haplotypes are rare, with a low frequency of occurrence.

Many people have common Haplotypes, which means that they would expect to find matches to those who do not have their surname. This occurs because we were all at one point related. As the different branches of the Adam +Eve tree evolved throughout time, mutations occurred, forming different Haplotypes. Thousands of years later, you have many different Haplotypes. Due to these mutations, you could have two branches that mutate to an identical Haplotype. This is called convergence.

If your Haplotype matches an individual with a different surname, and your genealogy research shows no evidence of an extra-marital event or adoption, your match may be the result of Convergence.

The example below shows convergence between the ABC surname and the XYZ surname, using just 3 markers to keep the example simple. Notice how the mutations over time bring two different Family Lines to the point that they match.

Time	ABC	XYZ
1000 A.D.	12 24 15	14 25 13
1200	13 24 15	14 25 13
1400	13 24 15	14 25 14
1600	13 24 15	14 24 14
1800	13 24 15	13 24 14
2000	13 24 14	13 24 14

Convergence explains why a haplotype will match others with a different surname. DNA testing for genealogy is not a substitute for genealogy research, but is instead a companion. Results that match must be considered in light of the genealogy research. If you match someone with a different surname, most likely there wasn't an adoption or extra marital event, and your match may be the result of convergence.

Case Studies in Genetic Genealogy

In each issue of the Newsletter, Family Tree DNA looks at what Genetic Genealogy will do for your Family History research. This article is a continuation of the topic, with situations, called "*Case Studies*", followed by a recommendation. The objective of the case studies is to present different situations you may encounter in your family history research, and how DNA testing can be applied.

Case Study

Reprinted with permission, from November 21, 2002 Volume 1, Issue 5, *Family Tree DNA Newsletter*, "I have participated in a Surname Project, and had quite surprising results. All the other Lines of my surname are related, except my Line. We have all traced our ancestors to England. Not only is my line not related, but also my ethnic origin is Eastern European. What do I do now?"

Recommendation

From November 21, 2002 Volume 1, Issue 5, *Family Tree DNA Newsletter*, " I am sure you were quite surprised, and perhaps disappointed. The first step is to validate the result for your Line or family tree. Since only one person was tested for your Line, we recommend testing additional males from each branch on your tree, to see if they all match each other. If they end up matching, your result is probably due to an extra marital event, an adoption, or a name or spelling change.

"In reviewing the surnames of Eastern Europe, your surname is pronounced as the surname in England, only the spelling is different. A review of your Family History shows that the research and documentation for the time period 1800-1850 is quite sparse. Many more records are available in England for this time period, including parish registers and wills. I would suggest that more family history research might shed some light on the situation."

     *   *   *

Chapter Twelve

Managing a Genetic Genealogy Project: Participants with Poor Documentation

Occasionally you might run across a willing participant for your Surname Project who has a poorly documented family tree, perhaps even built entirely out of the International Genealogical Index (IGI) by matching surnames. Your dilemma is that the prospective participant appears to be from a Line you haven't tested yet, but without better research you can't be sure. What comes first, the testing or the research?

This is a complex issue. If you turn away the participant and suggest that they do more research, they may become discouraged, and never return. If the participant tests, and gets unexpected results, they may become an unhappy participant.

One solution is to fill in the gaps of their research. You may not have the time to take this step. A better solution may be to communicate the situation to the participant, and let them make the decision to test now with the possibility of unexpected results, and also encourage them to do further research.

Perhaps from your research experience, you may be able to suggest to the participant specific sources for them to investigate. Most likely, they want to do more research, and just need some guidance and direction.

It will be a win-win for both the Surname Project and the participant if you are able to achieve both additional research on their part, and their participation.

Spot Light: Witt—Whitt Surname Project

Objective: Prove or disprove the genealogy research of the Witt / Whitt Line from Old Virginia

There are three identified Lines or families of the Witt / Whitt surname in the US. One family Line that today spells their surname as both Witt and Whitt begins with German immigrants in both South Carolina and Pennsylvania in the early 1700s. A second family Line that today spells their surname as Witt and DeWitt, began in New England around 1640 with an English immigrant by the name of John Witt.

The third family Line that today spells their surname as Witt and Whitt began with an individual named John Witt or Whitt, who first appears in early records in 1670 in colonial Virginia. The records relating to John show the spelling of his name both as Witt and as Whitt. It was from John Witt-Whitt that the Witt-Whitt Family of Old Virginia began.

Early Virginia records, John Witt-Whitt was the father of at least four sons, John Witt II, William Witt, Edward Whitt, and Richard Whitt. The participants in the Witt-Whitt Surname Project are all documented descendants of the 4 identified sons of John Witt-Whitt: John Witt II, William Witt, Edward Whitt, and Richard Whitt. For each of these sons, at least two documented male descendants participated in the Project. All participants took the 25 marker test.

The results for this Surname Project are that the majority of participants matched 25/25, and a few matched 24/25. Therefore, the Project has confirmed the genealogy research, and shows that the participants are related and have a common ancestor.

When combined with surviving colonial Virginia records for the surnames Witt and Whitt, the Witt-Whitt DNA study determined John Witt II, William Witt, Edward Whitt, and Richard Whitt were brothers and their father was the immigrant John Witt-Whitt of Charles City County, Virginia. The Witt-Whitt DNA Surname Project also identified the common ancestor of these four men was from England, or possibly Scotland.

A DNA baseline for the Witt-Whitt family of Old Virginia has now been established. Other descendants who have incomplete records, or where records no longer exist and preclude the determination of a family's origin, may take the 25 marker DNA test to determine if they are related to the Witt-Whitt Line from old Virginia.

If other descendants find that they match, they can contact one of the participants in the baseline study to share the Witt-Whitt family of Old Virginia ancestral history for their family line. The next phase of the Witt-Whitt surname project is to identify the county in England or Scotland from which John Witt-Whitt originated.

If you're interested in receiving Facts & Genes newsletter, feel free to contact the editor at Family Tree DNA with your comments, feedback, questions to be addressed, as well as suggestions for future articles. If you would like your Surname Project featured in their *Spotlight* column in a future issue, please send an email telling them about your project. If you are a Project Manager and can help others with tips or suggestions, please contact the editor: editor@familytreedna.com

Reprinted with permission of Family Tree DNA, from "Facts and Genes" Newsletter. Copyright 2002, Family Tree DNA.

Reprint Policy:

Family Tree DNA encourages the circulation of "Facts & Genes" by newsletters and lists providing that you credit the author, include their copyright information (Copyright 2002, Family Tree DNA), and cite "Facts & Genes" (http://www.familytreeDNA.com/facts_genes.asp) as the source.
November 21, 2002 Volume 1, Issue 5

* * *

Chapter Thirteen

Haplogroups and Markers

What's a Recessive Gene?

Sometimes a recessive gene is referred to as a form of a gene called a recessive allele. The recessive allele will not express itself if combined with a dominant allele. The recessive allele is expressed by a lower-case letter. Some traits may be caused by having two recessive alleles.

Markers

How many genetic markers can tell us something for various pairings between groups of people? Markers often are great for telling multiple groups apart. For example, one marker in particular can tell Africans apart from all the other groups, but that marker can't tell Europeans from East Asians. Scientists also will look at male Y chromosomes to study various markers.

Markers are different for various ethnic groups. However, there also is some overlap as peoples become mixed. A geneticist can tell the percentages of various races by looking at the markers, even though we have come to accept there really is no such thing as a particular race because of the diversity between peoples in any one race. However, you can still look at genetic markers to see various ethnic group traits for people who have been separated for thousands of years.

African-European	54 markers
African-East Asian	50 markers
African-Native American	50 markers
European-East Asian	45 markers
European-Native American	41 markers
East Asian-Native American	24 markers

What is a Haplogroup? How is it different from a Haplotype?

Your matrilineal or female ancestors inherit the same mtDNA sequences which form a haplogroup. Look at female lineages starting with your mtDNA haplogroup today. It will be the same haplogroup letter as your common ancestor with the same haplogroup letter who lived 21,000 years ago. You are looking at a connection from a single female ancestor to all your direct female line ancestors today.

The sequences within the haplogroup may be slightly different because of the slow mutation rate of the mtDNA, but the haplogroup will be the same. And in some cases, the sequences will be similar to your ancient ancestors. While in other cases, the mutation rate may have changed your mtDNA just a little over that long span of time.

What's a Haplotype?

Let's look at the female lineages, the mitochondrial DNA clues called mtDNA for short.

Individual mitochondrial DNA called for short, mtDNA sequences, is grouped into haplotypes. A haplotype defines a series of special mutations. The mutations when lumped together are called haplogroups. Each haplogroup contains a set of haplotypes descended from the same one common ancestor. How many haplogroups of mtDNA are there? According to Bryan Syke's book, *The Seven*

Daughters of Eve, at least 35 mtDNA haplogroups represented by a letter of the alphabet are listed in one of the illustrated tables. Matrilineal (female ancestral) lineages contain the mitochondria.

You can look at ancient ancestry by tracing the mtDNA lines. Some mtDNA letters belong mostly to Africa, while others belong to East Asia. Some are specific to South West Asia (India) and others are found in central and west Eurasia, which includes Europe and the Middle East. Five different mtDNA haplogroups are found in the New World—the Americas, such as ABCD and X, but the differences between the European and Middle Eastern X and the X among some Native American peoples show that they have been separated for thousands of years.

For example, in the book *Mapping Human History,* by Steve Olson, a rare and unusual haplogroup, X showed up among the Algonquian-speaking Native Americans living around the Great Lakes. It also is present in small amounts in the Lakota and Sioux.

Studies like this of X haplogroup mtDNA and other mtDNA haplogroups show up in articles collected in books such as *Archaeogenetics,* Edited by Colin Renfrew & Katie Boyle, McDonald Institute Monographs. See "Genetic Data and the Colonization of Europe," page 139-148 on "Founder Analysis."

Or see "The Topology of the Maternal Lineages of the Anatolian and Trans-Caucasus Populations and the Peopling of Europe: Some Preliminary Considerations, on page 219. Haplogroup X also appears in Russia. See the article on page 251, and similar studies. Also see Bryan Sykes book, The Seven Daughters of Eve for the section on Haplogroup X in the new world and in Europe. So mtDNA haplogroup X has really traveled across Europe and Asia in prehistoric times.

Previously mtDNA haplogroup X had been found in Finland, and in Italian, Greek, and Druze (Israel and Lebanon) peoples. Haplogroup X so far has not been found in East Asians. It's not found in modern Siberia. How did it get to the New World?

In both Sykes' book and in Olson's book, The Native American X mtDNA differed very much from the European haplogroup X to be separated by only one or two thousand years.

A recent video on ancestry broadcast on public TV showed a Greek woman standing next to a Native American. Both had mtDNA haplogroup X.

Did the Greek woman's X look exactly the same as the Native American man's? No. The Native American's haplogroup X had to have come to the New World tens of thousands of years ago. What happened? The Native American man's haplogroup X mtDNA was separated so many thousands of years from the European woman's haplogroup X mtDNA. Several changes occurred in both people's mtDNA during that long time of separation. Yet the two people still showed haplogroup X mtDNA.

As Steve Olson explains in his book, *Mapping Human History*, Scientist Douglas Wallace of the Center for Molecular Medicine at Emory University in Atlanta is one of the world's leading experts on mitochondrial genetics. So when he studied two skeletons that lived in the 1300s in Illinois among the Native Americans of that time, he found the skeletons contained traces of haplogroup X.

How did he know it wasn't from mixture with a European? It was the time divergence between the European and the Native American X haplogroup that gave the answer. The haplogroup X in North America had been there for more than 10,000 years. It wasn't a "modern" European who lived in Illinois in the 14th century.

Again, you might ask, perhaps it was a Viking from Finland since X is found in Finland? The tests showed this type of X differs from the European X by mutations that reveal the X that lived in America really had been there more than 10,000 years. So it could have come more than 10,000 years ago from anywhere—central Asia, Siberia. No X haplogroups are in Siberia today as far as one can tell.

Then again, not everyone has been tested there. However, you have to draw the line somewhere, and the differences between the old world and new world X haplogroup were great—as if they had been separated more than 10,000 years. It's easy to imagine someone in north central Asia could have joined up with a group of people such as hunters and traveled with them over the Bering Strait while it was still a land bridge more than 12,000 years ago.

What's a Haplogroup?

A group of related haplotypes make up a haplogroup. Haplogroups are studied especially when referring to mitochondrial DNA and Y-chromosomes. If a set of haplotypes are placed into a tree determined by the minimum number of mutations that separate them, the main branches of that tree are haplogroups. Each haplogroup in theory contains haplotypes that are all descended from a single founding individual.

Haplotypes from other regions of the genome are not studied as much because they may not always group together. Recombination makes ancestor-descendant relationships not as specific to see. You have to look for connections when you study haplotypes.

Examples: The vast majority of Native Americans belong to one of four mtDNA haplogroups: A, B, C, and D, but a few Native Americans also belong to haplogroup X. Haplogroup X is found at a low percentage in Europe, but the differences between the European haplogroup X and the Native American haplogroup X show that they separated more than 10,000 years ago.

It's more likely that someone with haplogroup X mtDNA from Southern Siberia, the Caucasus, or central Asia joined a group of hunters headed north and east more than 12,000 years ago when there was a land bridge over the Bering Strait, and settled in what is now called the North American continent.

* **What's an allele?**
For lots of definitions of these terms, also see the Web site: library.thinkquest.org/18258/noframes/def-allele.htm . Or See: *www.apnet.com/inscight/08271998/allele1.htm*

An allele is a form of a gene. Alleles are located at the same position (locus) on homologous chromosomes and are separated from each other during meiosis. An allele is what is actually within a region of the chromosome, and is found within a gene. An allele is *any of two or more alternative forms of a gene occupying the same chromosomal locus; such as that which determines flower petal color in peas.*

* **What's a Haplogroup?**
Definition: A bunch of haplotypes make up a haplogroup. The term is used usually when referring to female lineages and mitochondrial DNA or mtDNA. You might call a form of a gene an allele. An allele is an alternative form of a genetic locus. A single allele for each locus is inherited from each parent (e.g., at a locus for eye color the allele might result in blue or brown eyes).

So when a group of alleles on a single chromosome are linked together and usually inherited as a unit, these genes make up a haplogroup. Haplotypes are particularly stable in mitochondrial DNA and on the Y-chromosome, because they are not subject to recombination.

Analyses of mtDNA and Y-chromosome variation usually focus on the haplotype or haplogroup level, rather than comparing exact base pair sequences. In this case, haplotypes are defined on the basis of particular mutations shared by various individual DNA lineages.

Examples: One study of Finnish Y-chromosome variation found that 40% belonged to one of two different haplotypes, which in turn each belonged to different haplogroups and were probably introduced by different founding populations.

* **Genome.** A person's genome is one set of his (or her) genes. The human genes, which control a cell's structure, operation, and division, are located in the cell's nucleus. The full human genome (estimated at

50,000 to 100,000 genes) is present in every cell-nucleus. Many genes are inactive in cells that have some specialized functions. Many cells are differentiated to perform certain functions only.

* **Genes and Chromosomes.** Genes are composed of segments of DNA. In normal cell-nuclei, the DNA is distributed among 46 chromosomes (23 inherited at conception from a person's dad and 23 from mom). Each chromosome consists of one very long strand of DNA and numerous proteins.

The proteins are needed to manage the long DNA molecule. The longest chromosomes each support thousands of genes. Every time a cell divides, the cell must duplicate the 46 chromosomes. Every cell must distribute one copy of each chromosome to the two new cells. When cells stop dividing, that's the end of them and the organism.

* **The DNA Code.** The DNA of each chromosome is composed of units—"nucleotides" of four different types (A, T, G, C). These nucleotides are linked to each other in linear fashion. The necessary sequence of the four types of nucleotides produces the "code" which first determines the function of each particular gene. Then the sequence identifies the gene's start-point and stop-point along the DNA strand. Finally, the sequence allows specified regulatory functions. The code of the human genome consists of more than a billion nucleotides.

The Mitochondrial DNA (mtDNA). Mitochondria are needed for energy in the cell. The mitochondria are inherited from the mother. When tracing ancient and modern ancestry, geneticists look at female lineages or mtDNA. Your mtDNA is passed from mother to daughter over tens of thousands of years with few changes.

MtDNA mutates slowly during thousands of years of migrations of people across the globe. Men inherit their mtDNA from their mothers, but pass on their Y chromosomes to their sons. Women pass their mtDNA to their daughters. On very rare occasions, a few women may inherit some mtDNA from their fathers, but almost all women inherit their mtDNA from their mothers.

What mtDNA Does Not Do: It is not junk DNA. Often DNA produces more copies than it needs to function. Sometimes this is called junk DNA. MtDNA is necessary for providing energy to the cell. Outside the nucleus, human cells also have some "foreign" DNA located in structures called the mitochondria. This small and separate set of DNA does not participate in the 46 human chromosomes.

The mitochondrial DNA (mtDNA) really is not part of "the genomic DNA." According to the "out of Africa" theory that's widely held in acceptance by most scientists, all the mtDNA in the world today came from a single woman called Mitochondrial Eve who had two daughters who survived to create a line of females that expanded all over the world. Similar histories are noted for the male line using the Y chromosome. According to the book, *Mapping Human History*, by Steve Olson, (page 56) "All non-Africans descend from Africans who left the continent within the past 100,000 years."

According to a number of the latest videos on whether people took the northern or southern route out of Africa, the southern route is most favored. According to the book, *Archaeogenetics*, the flow of people varied between then and now. Today, most scientists theorize that since the north route out of Africa most likely was blocked by an Ice Age that created a dry desert in the Middle East, those leaving Africa headed toward Yemen and then along a southern route to India, Malaysia, and finally Australia.

Only when the climate changed and the Fertile Crescent of the Middle East opened up, did people expand back from India toward where the rivers met, the Middle East, such as what today are Iraq and Iran, and the Levant, reaching the coast, and from there north to what today is Europe. About 21,000 years ago, a new Ice Age began, and people who moved up from the Middle East into Europe found refuge in only a few places such as Southwest France, Northern Spain facing the Mediterranean and the Pyrenees, the Balkans and Ukraine, until the last

Ice Age ended about 12,500 years ago. Then populations expanded across Europe from Spain to the Urals.

By that time, the Far East had been populated for a long time, and Central Asia was the newest land to be seen. Then by 9,000 years ago, farmers from the Levant and Anatolia moved into Europe and introduced the idea of farming so that about 80 percent of Europeans today consist of the old Paleolithic hunters and about 20 to 26 percent from the more recent arrivals from the Middle East, the cereal belt grain farmers of the Neolithic era that started about 10,000 years ago in the Levant and Fertile Crescent of the Middle East.

Genealogy, history, folklore, oral history, memoirs writing, diary journaling, demography, anthropology, and archaeology are in the midst of a molecular revolution. Has archaeology become archaeogenetics? Actually, molecular genetics biotechnology is one more *tool* in the hands of the genealogist, historian, archaeologist, folklorist, prosopographer, onomasticist, demographer, videographer, anthropologist, or family historian. And that tool, molecular genetics, is used to untangle distantly ancestral as well as recent family roots.

Now you have computer technology and Web databases to research family ties. You have molecular genetics biotechnology—DNA testing, bioinformatics, and beyond.

From ancestry by DNA to racial percentages by markers and phenomics, experts can customize medicine or therapy to an individual's genes.

You can take a paternity test. Or find out whether you're related to a distant cousin you never met. Or you can study DNA as legal evidence. Your genes are used for matching bone marrow donors to recipients. The molecular revolution is enhancing research. From community colleges where students earn one or two-year certificates in biotechnology to perform DNA testing and bioinformatics processing on computers to the PhDs who work in research labs and universities, the molecular revolution has now joined science to history. How much do you want to know about your genome?

*   *   *

CHAPTER FOURTEEN

Have a Personal or Family History of Cancer? Consider Joining the Cancer Genetics Network

Reprinted with permission from the Cancer Genetics Network (CGN)

The Cancer Genetics Network (CGN) seeks individuals with a personal or family history of cancer who may be interested in participating in studies about inherited susceptibility to cancer. Nearly 8,500 individuals have enrolled in this unique program.

The Network is becoming an important vehicle to conduct studies that will provide much-needed clinical information to help individuals who may be at increased risk for cancer because of a personal or family history of the disease.

Eight U.S. centers, funded by the National Cancer Institute (NCI), joined forces 3 years ago to establish a national resource to support investigations into the genetic basis of cancer susceptibility. Together, the centers are working to make possible research that a single institution may not be able to accomplish because of insufficient numbers of participants, or the time needed to recruit them.

"The idea is to have a pool of interested individuals readily available so that important research questions can be answered, and studies can progress without unnecessary delay," said Deborah Winn, PhD, acting associate director of NCI's Epidemiology and Genetics Research Program (EGRP), Division of Cancer Control and Population Sciences (DCCPS). Participants may be invited to be part of specific studies, depending on the research requirements, and may choose to participate on a study-by-study basis.

Questions in Search of Answers

The Network's emphasis is on supporting research that brings the tremendous knowledge about genetics gained from laboratory research to bear on improving prevention, screening, diagnosis, and treatment of cancer in humans. "A wealth of new information on genetics has emerged over the past decade, and the challenge now is to find out how to make these findings meaningful in clinical practice and for public health programs," said Dr. Winn.

Some of the pressing questions that the Network aims to address are:
- How common are the genetic changes (alterations) that cause cancer in different groups?
- What determines whether someone with a genetic change gets cancer?
- What environmental exposures interact with genetic susceptibility to cause cancer?
- How can genetic discoveries be translated into better ways to prevent and treat cancer?
- What ethical, psychological, social, and family issues affect healthy individuals and their families who carry cancer susceptibility gene alterations?

"The Cancer Genetics Network is uniquely suited to support research centered on the study of key interactions between external environmental exposures and inherited susceptibility factors for cancer," said Joellen Schildkraut, Ph.D., of Duke University Medical Center, Durham, NC, and chair of the Network's Steering Committee. "This research can lead to the design of timely interventions, such as behavior modifications and chemoprevention strategies that prevent cancer or halt its progression."

Being Part of the Network

The Network offers individuals an opportunity to keep up to date on cancer genetics and potentially to participate in studies. All Network centers are enrolling eligible participants, and are especially interested in recruiting minorities, among whom membership lags. "We want all groups to be able to take advantage of this opportunity and to benefit from the studies," said Dr. Winn.

Participants provide information about their personal and family medical histories, which is entered into a central database that is operated by an informatics group. Presently, information on more than 134,000 family members is in the database. All information is kept private and is protected by the latest communications technology safeguards.

Network researchers and their centers have longstanding experience in working with individuals and families at increased risk for cancer, and will confidentially consult with individuals who are interested in joining. "The ultimate aim is to prevent cancer, and our best hope for developing effective cancer prevention programs lies in the early identification of high-risk populations and individuals at high risk," said Dr. Schildkraut.

Pilot Studies Under Way

Although still a young program, the Network is conducting a variety of pilot studies. It also has begun to work with other research groups, and welcomes new opportunities to cooperate on important research. Some of the pilot studies under way, or slated to begin soon, are to:
- Test the value of screening for ovarian cancer among women at high risk for the disease using a blood test for CA–125 (a chemical

found in the blood) and transvaginal ultrasound;
- Search for novel regions on genes associated with susceptibility to colon cancer among siblings who have a history of the disease;
- Obtain and characterize biological specimens from families who have a history of onset of prostate cancer at an early age;
- Study genetic and environmental factors that may modify risk for developing breast or ovarian cancer among women who are carriers of BRCA1 and BRCA2 gene alterations; and
- Compare statistical models for estimating the likelihood that a woman has a BRCA1 or BRCA2 gene alteration based on her family history.

How to Contact the Network

Individuals may contact one of the Network centers to discuss enrollment. It is not necessary to live near a center in order to join. Some centers have hospital affiliates through which one can enroll, and much of the contact can be by telephone, mail, or e-mail. More information about the Network is available on NCI's Web site: http://epi.grants.cancer.gov/CGN on the Internet.

Carolina-Georgia Cancer Genetics Network Center

Institutions:	Duke University Medical Center, Durham, NC, in collaboration with the University of North Carolina at Chapel Hill, NC, and Emory University, Atlanta, GA
Principal investigator:	Joellen Schildkraut, Ph.D., Duke University Medical Center
CGN Web site:	http://cancer.duke.edu/CGN

Institution: Duke University Medical Center
Contact: Sydnee Steadman
Telephone: 888–681–4762 (toll free)
E-mail: stead006@mc.duke.edu

Institution: University of North Carolina at Chapel Hill
Contact: Cindy Smith
Telephone: 877–692–6960 (toll free)
E-mail: cesmith@med.unc.edu

Institution: Emory University
Contact: Lisa Susswein
Telephone: 800–366–1502 (toll free)
E-mail: lrs@rw.ped.emory.edu

Georgetown University Medical Center's Cancer Genetics Network

Institution: Georgetown University Lombardi Cancer Center, Washington, DC
Principal investigator: Claudine Isaacs, M.D.
CGN Web site: http://lombardi.georgetown.edu/research/areas/cancercontrol/cgn
Contact: Camille Corio
Telephone: 202–687–8070
E-mail: corioc@georgetown.edu

Mid-Atlantic Cancer Genetics Network Center

Institutions:	Johns Hopkins University, Baltimore, MD, in collaboration with the Greater Baltimore Medical Center
Principal investigator:	Constance Griffin, M.D., Johns Hopkins University
CGN Web site:	http://www.macgn.org
Contact:	CGN Staff
Telephone:	877–880–6188 (toll free)

Northwest Cancer Genetics Network

Institutions:	Fred Hutchinson Cancer Research Center, Seattle, WA, in collaboration with the University of Washington School of Medicine, Seattle
Principal investigator:	John D. Potter, M.D., Ph.D., Fred Hutchinson Cancer Research Center
CGN Web site:	http://www.fhcrc.org/science/phs/cgn
Contact:	CGN Staff
Telephone:	800–616–8347 (toll free)

Rocky Mountain Cancer Genetics Coalition

Institutions:	University of Utah, Salt Lake City, UT, in collaboration with the University of Colorado, Aurora, CO, and University of New Mexico, Albuquerque, NM
Principal investigator:	Geraldine Mineau, Ph.D., University of Utah, Salt Lake City
CGN Web site:	http://www.hci.utah.edu/cgn

Institution:	University of Utah
Contact:	Debra Dutson
Telephone:	877–585–0473 (toll free)
E-mail:	ddutson@hci.utah.edu

Institution:	University of New Mexico
Contact:	Lloryn Swan
Telephone:	505–272–5659
E-mail:	swan@nmtr.unm.edu

Institution:	University of Colorado
Contact:	Theresa Mickiewicz
Telephone:	877–700–0697 (toll free)
E-mail:	theresa.mickiewicz@uchsc.edu

Texas Cancer Genetics Consortium

Institutions:	University of Texas M.D. Anderson Cancer Center, Houston, TX, in collaboration with the University of Texas Health Science Center at San Antonio, University of Texas Southwestern Medical Center at Dallas, and Baylor College of Medicine, Houston
Principal investigator:	Louise C. Strong, M.D., M.D. Anderson Cancer Center
CGN Web site:	http://texas.cgnweb.org
Telephone:	877-900-8894 (toll free)
Institution:	Baylor College of Medicine
Contact:	Sharon Plon, M.D.
Telephone:	713-770-4251
E-mail:	splon@bcm.tmc.edu
Institution:	University of Texas Southwestern Medical Center
Contact:	Gail Tomlinson, M.D.
Telephone:	214-648-4907
E-mail:	tomlinson@simmons.swmed.edu
Institution:	University of Texas Health Sciences Center
Contact:	Susan Naylor, M.D.
Telephone:	210-567-3842
E-mail:	naylor@uthscsa.edu
Institution:	University of Texas M.D. Anderson Cancer Center
Contact:	Louise C. Strong, M.D.

Telephone: 713–792–7555
E-mail: lstrong@mdanderson.org

UCI-UCSD Cancer Genetics Network Center

Institutions: University of California at Irvine and University of California at San Diego
Principal investigator: Hoda Anton-Culver, Ph.D., UC Irvine
Contact: CGN Staff
Telephone: 949–824–7401 (collect calls accepted)

IUniversity of Pennsylvania Cancer Genetics Network

Institution: University of Pennsylvania Cancer Center, Philadelphia, PA
Principal investigator: Barbara Weber, M.D.
Contact: Rhonda Kitlas
Telephone: 888–666–6002 (toll free)
E-mail: kitlasr@mail.med.upenn.edu

Informatics Infrastructure

The CGN also has an Informatics and Information Technology Group to meet its information exchange and data management and statistical needs. The participating institutions and principal investigators are the University of California at Irvine, with Hoda Anton-Culver, Ph.D.; Massachusetts General Hospital, Boston, MA, with Dianne M. Finkelstein, Ph.D.; and Yale University, New Haven, CT, with Prakash M. Nadkarni, Ph.D.

     #   #   #

Sources of National Cancer Institute Information

Cancer Information Service
 Toll-free: 1–800–4–CANCER (1–800–422–6237)
 TTY (for deaf and hard of hearing callers): 1–800–332–8615

NCI Online
 Internet
 Use http://cancer.gov to reach NCI's Web site.
 LiveHelp
 Cancer Information Specialists offer online assistance through the *LiveHelp* link on the NCI's Web site.

     *   *   *

CHAPTER FIFTEEN

Dictionary of Genetic Terms

Genomics and Its Impact on Medicine and Society: A 2001 Primer

Reprinted with permission of the US Dept. of Energy, Human Genome Program, Dictionary of Genetic Terms.
http://www.ornl.gov.hgmis

A

Acquired genetic mutation
See: somatic cell genetic mutation

Additive genetic effects
When the combined effects of alleles at different loci are equal to the sum of their individual effects.
See also: anticipation, complex trait

Adenine (A)
A nitrogenous base, one member of the base pair AT (adenine-thymine).
See also: base pair, nucleotide

Affected relative pair
Individuals related by blood, each of whom is affected with the same trait. Examples are affected sibling, cousin, and avuncular pairs.
See also: avuncular relationship

Aggregation technique
A technique used in model organism studies in which embryos at the 8-cell stage of development are pushed together to yield a single embryo (used as an alternative to microinjection).
See also: model organisms

Allele
Alternative form of a genetic locus; a single allele for each locus is inherited from each parent (e.g., at a locus for eye color the allele might result in blue or brown eyes).
See also: locus, gene expression

Allogeneic
Variation in alleles among members of the same species.

Alternative splicing
Different ways of combining a gene's exons to make variants of the complete protein

Amino acid
Any of a class of 20 molecules that are combined to form proteins in living things. The sequence of amino acids in a protein and hence protein function are determined by the genetic code.

Amplification
An increase in the number of copies of a specific DNA fragment; can be in vivo or in vitro.
See also: cloning, polymerase chain reaction

Animal model
See: model organisms

Annotation
Adding pertinent information such as gene coded for, amino acid sequence, or other commentary to the database entry of raw sequence of DNA bases.
See also: bioinformatics

Anticipation
Each generation of offspring has increased severity of a genetic disorder; e.g., a grandchild may have earlier onset and more severe symptoms than the parent, who had earlier onset than the grandparent.
See also: additive genetic effects, complex trait

Antisense
Nucleic acid that has a sequence exactly opposite to an mRNA molecule made by the body; binds to the mRNA molecule to prevent a protein from being made.
See also: transcription
Apoptosis
Programmed cell death, the body's normal method of disposing of damaged, unwanted, or unneeded cells.
See also: cell
Arrayed library
Individual primary recombinant clones (hosted in phage, cosmid, YAC, or other vector) that are placed in two-dimensional arrays in microtiter dishes. Each primary clone can be identified by the identity of the plate and the clone location (row and column) on that plate. Arrayed libraries of clones can be used for many applications, including screening for a specific gene or genomic region of interest.
See also: library, genomic library, gene chip technology
Assembly
Putting sequenced fragments of DNA into their correct chromosomal positions.
Autoradiography
A technique that uses X-ray film to visualize radioactively labeled molecules or fragments of molecules; used in analyzing length and number of DNA fragments after they are separated by gel electrophoresis.
Autosomal dominant
A gene on one of the non-sex chromosomes that is always expressed, even if only one copy is present. The chance of passing the gene to offspring is 50% for each pregnancy.
See also: autosome, dominant, gene

Autosome
A chromosome not involved in sex determination. The diploid human genome consists of a total of 46 chromosomes: 22 pairs of autosomes, and 1 pair of sex chromosomes (the X and Y chromosomes).
See also: sex chromosome

Avuncular relationship
The genetic relationship between nieces and nephews and their aunts and uncles.

B

Backcross
A cross between an animal that is heterozygous for alleles obtained from two parental strains and a second animal from one of those parental strains. Also used to describe the breeding protocol of an outcross followed by a backcross.
See also: model organisms

Bacterial artificial chromosome (BAC)
A vector used to clone DNA fragments (100- to 300-kb insert size; average, 150 kb) in *Escherichia coli* cells. Based on naturally occurring F-factor plasmid found in the bacterium *E. coli*.
See also: cloning vector

Bacteriophage
See: phage

Base
One of the molecules that form DNA and RNA molecules.
See also: nucleotide, base pair, base sequence

Base pair (bp)
Two nitrogenous bases (adenine and thymine or guanine and cytosine) held together by weak bonds. Two strands of DNA are held together in the shape of a double helix by the bonds between base pairs.

Base sequence
The order of nucleotide bases in a DNA molecule; determines structure of proteins encoded by that DNA.

Base sequence analysis
A method, sometimes automated, for determining the base sequence.

Behavioral genetics
The study of genes that may influence behavior.

Bioinformatics
The science of managing and analyzing biological data using advanced computing techniques. Especially important in analyzing genomic research data.
See also: informatics

Bioremediation
The use of biological organisms such as plants or microbes to aid in removing hazardous substances from an area.

Biotechnology
A set of biological techniques developed through basic research and now applied to research and product development. In particular, biotechnology refers to the use by industry of recombinant DNA, cell fusion, and new bioprocessing techniques.

Birth defect
Any harmful trait, physical or biochemical, present at birth, whether a result of a genetic mutation or some other nongenetic factor.
See also: congenital, gene, mutation, syndrome

BLAST
A computer program that identifies homologous (similar) genes in different organisms, such as human, fruit fly, or nematode.

C

Cancer
Diseases in which abnormal cells divide and grow unchecked. Cancer can spread from its original site to other parts of the body and can be fatal.
See also: hereditary cancer, sporadic cancer
Candidate gene
A gene located in a chromosome region suspected of being involved in a disease.
See also: positional cloning, protein
Capillary array
Gel-filled silica capillaries used to separate fragments for DNA sequencing. The small diameter of the capillaries permit the application of higher electric fields, providing high speed, high throughput separations that are significantly faster than traditional slab gels.
Carcinogen
Something which causes cancer to occur by causing changes in a cell's DNA.
See also: mutagene
Carrier
An individual who possesses an unexpressed, recessive trait.

cDNA library
A collection of DNA sequences that code for genes. The sequences are generated in the laboratory from mRNA sequences.
See also: messenger RNA

Cell
The basic unit of any living organism that carries on the biochemical processes of life.
See also: genome, nucleus

Centimorgan (cM)
A unit of measure of recombination frequency. One centimorgan is equal to a 1% chance that a marker at one genetic locus will be separated from a marker at a second locus due to crossing over in a single generation. In human beings, one centimorgan is equivalent, on average, to one million base pairs.
See also: megabase

Centromere
A specialized chromosome region to which spindle fibers attach during cell division.

Chimera (pl. chimaera)
An organism that contains cells or tissues with a different genotype. These can be mutated cells of the host organism or cells from a different organism or species.

Chimeraplasty
An experimental targeted repair process in which a desirable sequence of DNA is combined with RNA to form a chimeraplast. These molecules bind selectively to the target DNA. Once bound, the chimeraplast activates a naturally occurring gene-correcting mechanism. Does not use viral or other conventional gene-delivery vectors.
See also: gene therapy, cloning vector

Chloroplast chromosome
Circular DNA found in the photosynthesizing organelle (chloroplast) of plants instead of the cell nucleus where most genetic material is located.

Chromomere
One of the serially aligned beads or granules of a eukaryotic chromosome, resulting from local coiling of a continuous DNA thread.

Chromosomal deletion
The loss of part of a chromosome's DNA.

Chromosomal inversion
Chromosome segments that have been turned 180 degrees. The gene sequence for the segment is reversed with respect to the rest of the chromosome.

Chromosome
The self-replicating genetic structure of cells containing the cellular DNA that bears in its nucleotide sequence the linear array of genes. In prokaryotes, chromosomal DNA is circular, and the entire genome is carried on one chromosome. Eukaryotic genomes consist of a number of chromosomes whose DNA is associated with different kinds of proteins.

Chromosome painting
Attachment of certain fluorescent dyes to targeted parts of the chromosome. Used as a diagnositic for particular diseases, e.g. types of leukemia.

Chromosome region p
A designation for the short arm of a chromosome.

Chromosome region q
A designation for the long arm of a chromosome.

Clone
An exact copy made of biological material such as a DNA segment (e.g., a gene or other region), a whole cell, or a complete organism.

Clone bank
See: genomic library

Cloning
Using specialized DNA technology to produce multiple, exact copies of a single gene or other segment of DNA to obtain enough material

for further study. This process, used by researchers in the Human Genome Project, is referred to as cloning DNA. The resulting cloned (copied) collections of DNA molecules are called clone libraries. A second type of cloning exploits the natural process of cell division to make many copies of an entire cell. The genetic makeup of these cloned cells, called a cell line, is identical to the original cell. A third type of cloning produces complete, genetically identical animals such as the famous Scottish sheep, Dolly.

See also: cloning vector

Cloning vector

DNA molecule originating from a virus, a plasmid, or the cell of a higher organism into which another DNA fragment of appropriate size can be integrated without loss of the vector's capacity for self-replication; vectors introduce foreign DNA into host cells, where the DNA can be reproduced in large quantities. Examples are plasmids, cosmids, and yeast artificial chromosomes; vectors are often recombinant molecules containing DNA sequences from several sources.

Code

See: genetic code

Codominance

Situation in which two different alleles for a genetic trait are both expressed.

See also: autosomal dominant, recessive gene

Codon

See: genetic code

Coisogenic or congenic

Nearly identical strains of an organism; they vary at only a single locus.

Comparative genomics

The study of human genetics by comparisons with model organisms such as mice, the fruit fly, and the bacterium *E. coli*.

Complementary DNA (cDNA)
DNA that is synthesized in the laboratory from a messenger RNA template.

Complementary sequence
Nucleic acid base sequence that can form a double-stranded structure with another DNA fragment by following base-pairing rules (A pairs with T and C with G). The complementary sequence to GTAC for example, is CATG.

Complex trait
Trait that has a genetic component that does not follow strict Mendelian inheritance. May involve the interaction of two or more genes or gene-environment interactions.
See also: Mendelian inheritance, additive genetic effects

Computational biology
See: bioinformatics

Confidentiality
In genetics, the expectation that genetic material and the information gained from testing that material will not be available without the donor's consent.

Congenital
Any trait present at birth, whether the result of a genetic or nongenetic factor.
See also: birth defect

Conserved sequence
A base sequence in a DNA molecule (or an amino acid sequence in a protein) that has remained essentially unchanged throughout evolution.

Constitutive ablation
Gene expression that results in cell death.

Contig
Group of cloned (copied) pieces of DNA representing overlapping regions of a particular chromosome.

Contig map
A map depicting the relative order of a linked library of overlapping clones representing a complete chromosomal segment.

Cosmid
Artificially constructed cloning vector containing the cos gene of phage lambda. Cosmids can be packaged in lambda phage particles for infection into *E. coli*; this permits cloning of larger DNA fragments (up to 45kb) than can be introduced into bacterial hosts in plasmid vectors.

Crossing over
The breaking during meiosis of one maternal and one paternal chromosome, the exchange of corresponding sections of DNA, and the rejoining of the chromosomes. This process can result in an exchange of alleles between chromosomes.
See also: recombination

Cytogenetics
The study of the physical appearance of chromosomes.
See also: karyotype

Cytological band
An area of the chromosome that stains differently from areas around it.
See also: cytological map

Cytological map
A type of chromosome map whereby genes are located on the basis of cytological findings obtained with the aid of chromosome mutations.

Cytoplasmic (uniparental) inheritance
See: cytoplasmic trait

Cytoplasmic trait
A genetic characteristic in which the genes are found outside the nucleus, in chloroplasts or mitochondria. Results in offspring inheriting genetic material from only one parent.

Cytosine (C)
A nitrogenous base, one member of the base pair GC (guanine and cytosine) in DNA.
See also: base pair, nucleotide

D

Data warehouse
A collection of databases, data tables, and mechanisms to access the data on a single subject.

Deletion
A loss of part of the DNA from a chromosome; can lead to a disease or abnormality.
See also: chromosome, mutation

Deletion map
A description of a specific chromosome that uses defined mutations—specific deleted areas in the genome—as 'biochemical signposts,' or markers for specific areas.

Deoxyribonucleotide
See: nucleotide

Deoxyribose
A type of sugar that is one component of DNA (deoxyribonucleic acid).

Diploid
A full set of genetic material consisting of paired chromosomes, one from each parental set. Most animal cells except the gametes have a diploid set of chromosomes. The diploid human genome has 46 chromosomes.
See also: haploid

Directed evolution
A laboratory process used on isolated molecules or microbes to cause mutations and identify subsequent adaptations to novel environments.

Directed mutagenesis
Alteration of DNA at a specific site and its reinsertion into an organism to study any effects of the change.

Directed sequencing
Successively sequencing DNA from adjacent stretches of chromosome.

Disease-associated genes
Alleles carrying particular DNA sequences associated with the presence of disease.

DNA (deoxyribonucleic acid)
The molecule that encodes genetic information. DNA is a double-stranded molecule held together by weak bonds between base pairs of nucleotides. The four nucleotides in DNA contain the bases adenine (A), guanine (G), cytosine (C), and thymine (T). In nature, base pairs form only between A and T and between G and C; thus the base sequence of each single strand can be deduced from that of its partner.

DNA bank
A service that stores DNA extracted from blood samples or other human tissue.

DNA probe
See: probe

DNA repair genes
Genes encoding proteins that correct errors in DNA sequencing.

DNA replication
The use of existing DNA as a template for the synthesis of new DNA strands. In humans and other eukaryotes, replication occurs in the cell nucleus.

DNA sequence
The relative order of base pairs, whether in a DNA fragment, gene, chromosome, or an entire genome.
See also: base sequence analysis

Domain
A discrete portion of a protein with its own function. The combination of domains in a single protein determines its overall function.

Dominant
An allele that is almost always expressed, even if only one copy is present.
See also: gene, genome

Double helix
The twisted-ladder shape that two linear strands of DNA assume when complementary nucleotides on opposing strands bond together.

Draft sequence
The sequence generated by the HGP as of June 2000 that, while incomplete, offers a virtual road map to an estimated 95% of all human genes. Draft sequence data are mostly in the form of 10,000 base pair-sized fragments whose approximate chromosomal locations are known.
See also: sequencing, finished DNA sequence, working draft DNA sequence.

E

Electrophoresis
A method of separating large molecules (such as DNA fragments or proteins) from a mixture of similar molecules. An electric current is passed through a medium containing the mixture, and each kind of molecule travels through the medium at a different rate, depending on its electrical charge and size. Agarose and acrylamide gels are the media commonly used for electrophoresis of proteins and nucleic acids.

Electroporation
A process using high-voltage current to make cell membranes permeable to allow the introduction of new DNA; commonly used in recombinant DNA technology.
See also: transfection

Embryonic stem (ES) cells
An embryonic cell that can replicate indefinitely, transform into other types of cells, and serve as a continuous source of new cells.

Endonuclease
See: restriction enzyme

Enzyme
A protein that acts as a catalyst, speeding the rate at which a biochemical reaction proceeds but not altering the direction or nature of the reaction.

Epistasis
One gene interferes with or prevents the expression of another gene located at a different locus.

Escherichia coli
Common bacterium that has been studied intensively by geneticists because of its small genome size, normal lack of pathogenicity, and ease of growth in the laboratory.

Eugenics
The study of improving a species by artificial selection; usually refers to the selective breeding of humans.

Eukaryote
Cell or organism with membrane-bound, structurally discrete nucleus and other well-developed subcellular compartments. Eukaryotes include all organisms except viruses, bacteria, and blue-green algae.
See also: prokaryote, chromosome.

Evolutionarily conserved
See: conserved sequence

Exogenous DNA
DNA originating outside an organism that has been introduced into the organism.

Exon
The protein-coding DNA sequence of a gene.
See also: intron

Exonuclease
An enzyme that cleaves nucleotides sequentially from free ends of a linear nucleic acid substrate.

Expressed gene
See: gene expression

Expressed sequence tag (EST)
A short strand of DNA that is a part of a cDNA molecule and can act as identifier of a gene. Used in locating and mapping genes.
See also: cDNA, sequence tagged site

F

Filial generation (F1, F2)
Each generation of offspring in a breeding program, designated F1, F2, etc.

Fingerprinting
In genetics, the identification of multiple specific alleles on a person's DNA to produce a unique identifier for that person.
See also: forensics

Finished DNA Sequence
High-quality, low error, gap-free DNA sequence of the human genome. Achieving this ultimate 2003 HGP goal requires additional sequencing to close gaps, reduce ambiguities, and allow for only a single error every 10,000 bases, the agreed-upon standard for HGP finished sequence.
See also: sequencing, draft sequence

Flow cytometry
Analysis of biological material by detection of the light-absorbing or fluorescing properties of cells or subcellular fractions (i.e., chromosomes) passing in a narrow stream through a laser beam. An absorbance or fluorescence profile of the sample is produced. Automated sorting devices, used to fractionate samples, sort successive droplets of the analyzed stream into different fractions depending on the fluorescence emitted by each droplet.

Flow karyotyping
Use of flow cytometry to analyze and separate chromosomes according to their DNA content.

Fluorescence in situ hybridization (FISH)
A physical mapping approach that uses fluorescein tags to detect hybridization of probes with metaphase chromosomes and with the less-condensed somatic interphase chromatin.

Forensics
The use of DNA for identification. Some examples of DNA use are to establish paternity in child support cases; establish the presence of a suspect at a crime scene, and identify accident victims.

Fraternal twin

Siblings born at the same time as the result of fertilization of two ova by two sperm. They share the same genetic relationship to each other as any other siblings.
See also: identical twin

Full gene sequence
The complete order of bases in a gene. This order determines which protein a gene will produce.

Functional genomics
The study of genes, their resulting proteins, and the role played by the proteins the body's biochemical processes.

G

Gamete
Mature male or female reproductive cell (sperm or ovum) with a haploid set of chromosomes (23 for humans).

GC-rich area
Many DNA sequences carry long stretches of repeated G and C which often indicate a gene-rich region.

Gel electrophoresis
See: electrophoresis

Gene
The fundamental physical and functional unit of heredity. A gene is an ordered sequence of nucleotides located in a particular position on a particular chromosome that encodes a specific functional product (i.e., a protein or RNA molecule).
See also: gene expression

Gene amplification
Repeated copying of a piece of DNA; a characteristic of tumor cells.
See also: gene, oncogene

Gene chip technology

Development of cDNA microarrays from a large number of genes. Used to monitor and measure changes in gene expression for each gene represented on the chip.

Gene expression

The process by which a gene's coded information is converted into the structures present and operating in the cell. Expressed genes include those that are transcribed into mRNA and then translated into protein and those that are transcribed into RNA but not translated into protein (e.g., transfer and ribosomal RNAs).

Gene family

Group of closely related genes that make similar products.

Gene library

See: genomic library

Gene mapping

Determination of the relative positions of genes on a DNA molecule (chromosome or plasmid) and of the distance, in linkage units or physical units, between them.

Gene pool

All the variations of genes in a species.

See also: allele, gene, polymorphism

Gene prediction

Predictions of possible genes made by a computer program based on how well a stretch of DNA sequence matches known gene sequences

Gene product

The biochemical material, either RNA or protein, resulting from expression of a gene. The amount of gene product is used to measure how active a gene is; abnormal amounts can be correlated with disease-causing alleles.

Gene testing

See: genetic testing, genetic screening

Gene therapy
An experimental procedure aimed at replacing, manipulating, or supplementing nonfunctional or misfunctioning genes with healthy genes.
See also: gene, inherit, somatic cell gene therapy, germ line gene therapy

Gene transfer
Incorporation of new DNA into and organism's cells, usually by a vector such as a modified virus. Used in gene therapy.
See also: mutation, gene therapy, vector

Genetic code
The sequence of nucleotides, coded in triplets (codons) along the mRNA, that determines the sequence of amino acids in protein synthesis. A gene's DNA sequence can be used to predict the mRNA sequence, and the genetic code can in turn be used to predict the amino acid sequence.

Genetic counseling
Provides patients and their families with education and information about genetic-related conditions and helps them make informed decisions.

Genetic discrimination
Prejudice against those who have or are likely to develop an inherited disorder.

Genetic engineering
Altering the genetic material of cells or organisms to enable them to make new substances or perform new functions.

Genetic engineering technology
See: recombinant DNA technology

Genetic illness
Sickness, physical disability, or other disorder resulting from the inheritance of one or more deleterious alleles.

Genetic informatics
 See: bioinformatics
Genetic map
 See: linkage map
Genetic marker
 A gene or other identifiable portion of DNA whose inheritance can be followed.
 See also: chromosome, DNA, gene, inherit
Genetic material
 See: genome
Genetic mosaic
 An organism in which different cells contain different genetic sequence. This can be the result of a mutation during development or fusion of embryos at an early developmental stage.
Genetic polymorphism
 Difference in DNA sequence among individuals, groups, or populations (e.g., genes for blue eyes versus brown eyes).
Genetic predisposition
 Susceptibility to a genetic disease. May or may not result in actual development of the disease.
Genetic screening
 Testing a group of people to identify individuals at high risk of having or passing on a specific genetic disorder.
Genetic testing
 Analyzing an individual's genetic material to determine predisposition to a particular health condition or to confirm a diagnosis of genetic disease.
Genetics
 The study of inheritance patterns of specific traits.
Genome
 All the genetic material in the chromosomes of a particular organism; its size is generally given as its total number of base pairs.

Genome project
   Research and technology-development effort aimed at mapping and sequencing the genome of human beings and certain model organisms.
   See also: Human Genome Initiative
Genomic library
   A collection of clones made from a set of randomly generated overlapping DNA fragments that represent the entire genome of an organism.
   See also: library, arrayed library
Genomic sequence
   See: DNA
Genomics
   The study of genes and their function.
Genotype
   The genetic constitution of an organism, as distinguished from its physical appearance (its phenotype).
Germ cell
   Sperm and egg cells and their precursors. Germ cells are haploid and have only one set of chromosomes (23 in all), while all other cells have two copies (46 in all).
Germ line
   The continuation of a set of genetic information from one generation to the next.
   See also: inherit
Germ line gene therapy
   An experimental process of inserting genes into germ cells or fertilized eggs to cause a genetic change that can be passed on to offspring. May be used to alleviate effects associated with a genetic disease.
   See also: genomics, somatic cell gene therapy.
Germ line genetic mutation
   See: mutation

Guanine (G)
A nitrogenous base, one member of the base pair GC (guanine and cytosine) in DNA.
See also: base pair, nucleotide

Gyandromorph
Organisms that have both male and female cells and therefore express both male and female characteristics.

H

Haploid
A single set of chromosomes (half the full set of genetic material) present in the egg and sperm cells of animals and in the egg and pollen cells of plants. Human beings have 23 chromosomes in their reproductive cells.
See also: diploid

Haplotype
A way of denoting the collective genotype of a number of closely linked loci on a chromosome.

Hemizygous
Having only one copy of a particular gene. For example, in humans, males are hemizygous for genes found on the Y chromosome.

Hereditary cancer
Cancer that occurs due to the inheritance of an altered gene within a family.
See also: sporadic cancer

Heterozygosity
The presence of different alleles at one or more loci on homologous chromosomes.

Heterozygote
See: heterozygosity

Highly conserved sequence
DNA sequence that is very similar across several different types of organisms.
See also: gene, mutation

High-throughput sequencing
A fast method of determining the order of bases in DNA.
See also: sequencing

Homeobox
A short stretch of nucleotides whose base sequence is virtually identical in all the genes that contain it. Homeoboxes have been found in many organisms from fruit flies to human beings. In the fruit fly, a homeobox appears to determine when particular groups of genes are expressed during development.

Homolog
A member of a chromosome pair in diploid organisms or a gene that has the same origin and functions in two or more species.

Homologous chromosome
Chromosome containing the same linear gene sequences as another, each derived from one parent.

Homologous recombination
Swapping of DNA fragments between paired chromosomes.

Homology
Similarity in DNA or protein sequences between individuals of the same species or among different species.

Homozygote
An organism that has two identical alleles of a gene.
See also: heterozygote

Homozygous
See: homozygote

Human artificial chromosome (HAC)
A vector used to hold large DNA fragments.

See also: chromosome, DNA
Human gene therapy
See: gene therapy
Human Genome Initiative
Collective name for several projects begun in 1986 by DOE to create an ordered set of DNA segments from known chromosomal locations, develop new computational methods for analyzing genetic map and DNA sequence data, and develop new techniques and instruments for detecting and analyzing DNA. This DOE initiative is now known as the Human Genome Program. The joint national effort, led by DOE and NIH, is known as the Human Genome Project.
Human Genome Project (HGP)
Formerly titled Human Genome Initiative.
See also: Human Genome Initiative
Hybrid
The offspring of genetically different parents.
See also: heterozygote
Hybridization
The process of joining two complementary strands of DNA or one each of DNA and RNA to form a double-stranded molecule.

I

Identical twin
Twins produced by the division of a single zygote; both have identical genotypes.
See also: fraternal twin
Immunotherapy
Using the immune system to treat disease, for example, in the development of vaccines. May also refer to the therapy of diseases caused by the immune system.
See also: cancer

Imprinting
A phenomenon in which the disease phenotype depends on which parent passed on the disease gene. For instance, both Prader-Willi and Angelman syndromes are inherited when the same part of chromosome 15 is missing. When the father's complement of 15 is missing, the child has Prader-Willi, but when the mother's complement of 15 is missing, the child has Angelman syndrome.

In situ hybridization
Use of a DNA or RNA probe to detect the presence of the complementary DNA sequence in cloned bacterial or cultured eukaryotic cells.

In vitro
Studies performed outside a living organism such as in a laboratory.

In vivo
Studies carried out in living organisms.

Independent assortment
During meiosis each of the two copies of a gene is distributed to the germ cells independently of the distribution of other genes.
See also: linkage

Informatics
See: bioinformatics

Informed consent
An individual willingly agrees to participate in an activity after first being advised of the risks and benefits.
See also: privacy

Inherit
In genetics, to receive genetic material from parents through biological processes.

Inherited
See: inherit

Insertion
A chromosome abnormality in which a piece of DNA is incorporated into a gene and thereby disrupts the gene's normal function.
See also: chromosome, DNA, gene, mutation

Insertional mutation
See: insertion

Intellectual property rights
Patents, copyrights, and trademarks.
See also: patent

Interference
One crossover event inhibits the chances of another crossover event. Also known as positive interference. Negative interference increases the chance of a second crossover.
See also: crossing over

Interphase
The period in the cell cycle when DNA is replicated in the nucleus; followed by mitosis.

Intron
DNA sequence that interrupts the protein-coding sequence of a gene; an intron is transcribed into RNA but is cut out of the message before it is translated into protein.
See also: exon

Isoenzyme
An enzyme performing the same function as another enzyme but having a different set of amino acids. The two enzymes may function at different speeds.

J

Junk DNA
Stretches of DNA that do not code for genes; most of the genome consists of so-called junk DNA which may have regulatory and other functions. Also called non-coding DNA.

K

Karyotype
A photomicrograph of an individual's chromosomes arranged in a standard format showing the number, size, and shape of each chromosome type; used in low-resolution physical mapping to correlate gross chromosomal abnormalities with the characteristics of specific diseases.

Kilobase (kb)
Unit of length for DNA fragments equal to 1000 nucleotides.

Knockout
Deactivation of specific genes; used in laboratory organisms to study gene function.
See also: gene, locus, model organisms

L

Library
An unordered collection of clones (i.e., cloned DNA from a particular organism) whose relationship to each other can be established by physical mapping.
See also: genomic library, arrayed library

Linkage
The proximity of two or more markers (e.g., genes, RFLP markers) on a chromosome; the closer the markers, the lower the probability that they will be separated during DNA repair or replication processes (binary fission in prokaryotes, mitosis or meiosis in eukaryotes), and hence the greater the probability that they will be inherited together.

Linkage disequilibrium
Where alleles occur together more often than can be accounted for by chance. Indicates that the two alleles are physically close on the DNA strand.
See also: Mendelian inheritance

Linkage map
A map of the relative positions of genetic loci on a chromosome, determined on the basis of how often the loci are inherited together. Distance is measured in centimorgans (cM).

Localize
Determination of the original position (locus) of a gene or other marker on a chromosome.

Locus (pl. loci)
The position on a chromosome of a gene or other chromosome marker; also, the DNA at that position. The use of locus is sometimes restricted to mean expressed DNA regions.
See also: gene expression

Long-Range Restriction Mapping
Restriction enzymes are proteins that cut DNA at precise locations. Restriction maps depict the chromosomal positions of restriction-enzyme cutting sites. These are used as biochemical "signposts," or markers of specific areas along the chromosomes. The map will detail the positions where the DNA molecule is cut by particular restriction enzymes.

M

Macrorestriction map
　Map depicting the order of and distance between sites at which restriction enzymes cleave chromosomes.

Mapping
　See: gene mapping, linkage map, physical map

Mapping population
　The group of related organisms used in constructing a genetic map.

Marker
　See: genetic marker

Mass spectrometry
　An instrument used to identify chemicals in a substance by their mass and charge.

Megabase (Mb)
　Unit of length for DNA fragments equal to 1 million nucleotides and roughly equal to 1 cM.
　See also: centimorgan

Meiosis
　The process of two consecutive cell divisions in the diploid progenitors of sex cells. Meiosis results in four rather than two daughter cells, each with a haploid set of chromosomes.
　See also: mitosis

Mendelian inheritance
　One method in which genetic traits are passed from parents to offspring. Named for Gregor Mendel, who first studied and recognized the existence of genes and this method of inheritance.
　See also: autosomal dominant, recessive gene, sex-linked

Messenger RNA (mRNA)
　RNA that serves as a template for protein synthesis.
　See also: genetic code

Metaphase
A stage in mitosis or meiosis during which the chromosomes are aligned along the equatorial plane of the cell.

Microarray
Sets of miniaturized chemical reaction areas that may also be used to test DNA fragments, antibodies, or proteins.

Microbial genetics
The study of genes and gene function in bacteria, archaea, and other microorganisms. Often used in research in the fields of bioremediation, alternative energy, and disease prevention.
See also: model organisms, biotechnology, bioremediation

Microinjection
A technique for introducing a solution of DNA into a cell using a fine microcapillary pipet.

Micronuclei
Chromosome fragments that are not incorporated into the nucleus at cell division.

Mitochondrial DNA
The genetic material found in mitochondria, the organelles that generate energy for the cell. Not inherited in the same fashion as nucleic DNA.
See also: cell, DNA, genome, nucleus

Mitosis
The process of nuclear division in cells that produces daughter cells that are genetically identical to each other and to the parent cell.
See also: meiosis

Model organisms
A laboratory animal or other organism useful for research.

Modeling
The use of statistical analysis, computer analysis, or model organisms to predict outcomes of research.

Molecular biology
The study of the structure, function, and makeup of biologically important molecules.

Molecular farming
The development of transgenic animals to produce human proteins for medical use.

Molecular genetics
The study of macromolecules important in biological inheritance.

Molecular medicine
The treatment of injury or disease at the molecular level. Examples include the use of DNA-based diagnostic tests or medicine derived from DNA sequence information.

Monogenic disorder
A disorder caused by mutation of a single gene.
See also: mutation, polygenic disorder

Monogenic inheritance
See: monogenic disorder

Monosomy
Possessing only one copy of a particular chromosome instead of the normal two copies.
See also: cell, chromosome, gene expression, trisomy

Morbid map
A diagram showing the chromosomal location of genes associated with disease.

Mouse model
See: model organisms

Multifactorial or multigenic disorder
See: polygenic disorder

Multiplexing
A laboratory approach that performs multiple sets of reactions in parallel (simultaneously); greatly increasing speed and throughput.

Murine
Organism in the genus Mus. A rat or mouse.

Mutagen
An agent that causes a permanent genetic change in a cell. Does not include changes occurring during normal genetic recombination.

Mutagenicity
The capacity of a chemical or physical agent to cause permanent genetic alterations.
See also: somatic cell genetic mutation

Mutation
Any heritable change in DNA sequence.
See also: polymorphism

N

Nitrogenous base
A nitrogen-containing molecule having the chemical properties of a base. DNA contains the nitrogenous bases adenine (A), guanine (G), cytosine (C), and thymine (T).
See also: DNA

Northern blot
A gel-based laboratory procedure that locates mRNA sequences on a gel that are complementary to a piece of DNA used as a probe.
See also: DNA, library

Nuclear transfer
A laboratory procedure in which a cell's nucleus is removed and placed into an oocyte with its own nucleus removed so the genetic

information from the donor nucleus controls the resulting cell. Such cells can be induced to form embryos. This process was used to create the cloned sheep "Dolly".
See also: cloning

Nucleic acid
A large molecule composed of nucleotide subunits.
See also: DNA

Nucleolar organizing region
A part of the chromosome containing rRNA genes.

Nucleotide
A subunit of DNA or RNA consisting of a nitrogenous base (adenine, guanine, thymine, or cytosine in DNA; adenine, guanine, uracil, or cytosine in RNA), a phosphate molecule, and a sugar molecule (deoxyribose in DNA and ribose in RNA). Thousands of nucleotides are linked to form a DNA or RNA molecule.
See also: DNA, base pair, RNA

Nucleus
The cellular organelle in eukaryotes that contains most of the genetic material.

O

Oligo
See: oligonucleotide

Oligogenic
A phenotypic trait produced by two or more genes working together.
See also: polygenic disorder

Oligonucleotide
A molecule usually composed of 25 or fewer nucleotides; used as a DNA synthesis primer.
See also: nucleotide

Oncogene
A gene, one or more forms of which is associated with cancer. Many oncogenes are involved, directly or indirectly, in controlling the rate of cell growth.

Open reading frame (ORF)
The sequence of DNA or RNA located between the start-code sequence (initiation codon) and the stop-code sequence (termination codon).

Operon
A set of genes transcribed under the control of an operator gene.

Overlapping clones
See: genomic library

P

P1-derived artificial chromosome (PAC)
One type of vector used to clone DNA fragments (100- to 300-kb insert size; average, 150 kb) in *Escherichia coli* cells. Based on bacteriophage (a virus) P1 genome.
See also: cloning vector

Patent
In genetics, conferring the right or title to genes, gene variations, or identifiable portions of sequenced genetic material to an individual or organization.
See also: gene

Pedigree
A family tree diagram that shows how a particular genetic trait or disease has been inherited.
See also: inherit

Penetrance

The probability of a gene or genetic trait being expressed. "Complete" penetrance means the gene or genes for a trait are expressed in all the population who have the genes. "Incomplete" penetrance means the genetic trait is expressed in only part of the population. The percent penetrance also may change with the age range of the population.

Peptide
Two or more amino acids joined by a bond called a "peptide bond."
See also: polypeptide

Phage
A virus for which the natural host is a bacterial cell.

Pharmacogenomics
The study of the interaction of an individual's genetic makeup and response to a drug.

Phenocopy
A trait not caused by inheritance of a gene but appears to be identical to a genetic trait.

Phenotype
The physical characteristics of an organism or the presence of a disease that may or may not be genetic.
See also: genotype

Physical map
A map of the locations of identifiable landmarks on DNA (e.g., restriction-enzyme cutting sites, genes), regardless of inheritance. Distance is measured in base pairs. For the human genome, the lowest-resolution physical map is the banding patterns on the 24 different chromosomes; the highest-resolution map is the complete nucleotide sequence of the chromosomes.

Plasmid
Autonomously replicating extra-chromosomal circular DNA molecules, distinct from the normal bacterial genome and nonessential for cell survival under nonselective conditions. Some plasmids are capable of integrating into the host genome. A number of artificially constructed plasmids are used as cloning vectors.

Pleiotropy
One gene that causes many different physical traits such as multiple disease symptoms.

Pluripotency
The potential of a cell to develop into more than one type of mature cell, depending on environment.

Polygenic disorder
Genetic disorder resulting from the combined action of alleles of more than one gene (e.g., heart disease, diabetes, and some cancers). Although such disorders are inherited, they depend on the simultaneous presence of several alleles; thus the hereditary patterns usually are more complex than those of single-gene disorders.
See also: single-gene disorder

Polymerase chain reaction (PCR)
A method for amplifying a DNA base sequence using a heat-stable polymerase and two 20-base primers, one complementary to the (+) strand at one end of the sequence to be amplified and one complementary to the (-) strand at the other end. Because the newly synthesized DNA strands can subsequently serve as additional templates for the same primer sequences, successive rounds of primer annealing, strand elongation, and dissociation produce rapid and highly specific amplification of the desired sequence. PCR also can be used to detect the existence of the defined sequence in a DNA sample.

Polymerase, DNA or RNA
Enzyme that catalyzes the synthesis of nucleic acids on preexisting nucleic acid templates, assembling RNA from ribonucleotides or DNA from deoxyribonucleotides.

Polymorphism
Difference in DNA sequence among individuals that may underlie differences in health. Genetic variations occurring in more than 1% of a population would be considered useful polymorphisms for genetic linkage analysis.
See also: mutation

Polypeptide
A protein or part of a protein made of a chain of amino acids joined by a peptide bond.

Population genetics
The study of variation in genes among a group of individuals.

Positional cloning
A technique used to identify genes, usually those that are associated with diseases, based on their location on a chromosome.

Premature chromosome condensation (PCC)
A method of studying chromosomes in the interphase stage of the cell cycle.

Primer
Short preexisting polynucleotide chain to which new deoxyribonucleotides can be added by DNA polymerase.

Privacy
In genetics, the right of people to restrict access to their genetic information.

Probe
Single-stranded DNA or RNA molecules of specific base sequence, labeled either radioactively or immunologically, that are used to detect the complementary base sequence by hybridization.

Prokaryote
Cell or organism lacking a membrane-bound, structurally discrete nucleus and other subcellular compartments. Bacteria are examples of prokaryotes.
See also: chromosome, eukaryote

Promoter
A DNA site to which RNA polymerase will bind and initiate transcription.

Pronucleus
The nucleus of a sperm or egg prior to fertilization.
See also: nucleus, transgenic

Protein
A large molecule composed of one or more chains of amino acids in a specific order; the order is determined by the base sequence of nucleotides in the gene that codes for the protein. Proteins are required for the structure, function, and regulation of the body's cells, tissues, and organs; and each protein has unique functions. Examples are hormones, enzymes, and antibodies.

Proteome
Proteins expressed by a cell or organ at a particular time and under specific conditions.

Proteomics
The study of the full set of proteins encoded by a genome.

Pseudogene
A sequence of DNA similar to a gene but nonfunctional; probably the remnant of a once-functional gene that accumulated mutations.

Purine
A nitrogen-containing, double-ring, basic compound that occurs in nucleic acids. The purines in DNA and RNA are adenine and guanine.
See also: base pair

Pyrimidine

A nitrogen-containing, single-ring, basic compound that occurs in nucleic acids. The pyrimidines in DNA are cytosine and thymine; in RNA, cytosine and uracil.

See also: base pair

R

Radiation hybrid

A hybrid cell containing small fragments of irradiated human chromosomes. Maps of irradiation sites on chromosomes for the human, rat, mouse, and other genomes provide important markers, allowing the construction of very precise STS maps indispensable to studying multifactorial diseases.

See also: sequence tagged site

Rare-cutter enzyme

See: restriction-enzyme cutting site

Recessive gene

A gene which will be expressed only if there are 2 identical copies or, for a male, if one copy is present on the X chromosome.

Reciprocal translocation

When a pair of chromosomes exchange exactly the same length and area of DNA. Results in a shuffling of genes.

Recombinant clone

Clone containing recombinant DNA molecules.

See also: recombinant DNA technology

Recombinant DNA molecules

A combination of DNA molecules of different origin that are joined using recombinant DNA technologies.

Recombinant DNA technology
Procedure used to join together DNA segments in a cell-free system (an environment outside a cell or organism). Under appropriate conditions, a recombinant DNA molecule can enter a cell and replicate there, either autonomously or after it has become integrated into a cellular chromosome.

Recombination
The process by which progeny derive a combination of genes different from that of either parent. In higher organisms, this can occur by crossing over.
See also: crossing over, mutation

Regulatory region or sequence
A DNA base sequence that controls gene expression.

Repetitive DNA
Sequences of varying lengths that occur in multiple copies in the genome; it represents much of the human genome.

Reporter gene
See: marker

Resolution
Degree of molecular detail on a physical map of DNA, ranging from low to high.

Restriction enzyme, endonuclease
A protein that recognizes specific, short nucleotide sequences and cuts DNA at those sites. Bacteria contain over 400 such enzymes that recognize and cut more than 100 different DNA sequences.
See also: restriction enzyme cutting site

Restriction fragment length polymorphism (RFLP)
Variation between individuals in DNA fragment sizes cut by specific restriction enzymes; polymorphic sequences that result in RFLPs are used as markers on both physical maps and genetic linkage maps. RFLPs usually are caused by mutation at a cutting site.
See also: marker, polymorphism

Restriction-enzyme cutting site
A specific nucleotide sequence of DNA at which a particular restriction enzyme cuts the DNA. Some sites occur frequently in DNA (e.g., every several hundred base pairs); others much less frequently (rare-cutter; e.g., every 10,000 base pairs).

Retroviral infection
The presence of retroviral vectors, such as some viruses, which use their recombinant DNA to insert their genetic material into the chromosomes of the host's cells. The virus is then propogated by the host cell.

Reverse transcriptase
An enzyme used by retroviruses to form a complementary DNA sequence (cDNA) from their RNA. The resulting DNA is then inserted into the chromosome of the host cell.

Ribonucleotide
See: nucleotide

Ribose
The five-carbon sugar that serves as a component of RNA.
See also: ribonucleic acid, deoxyribose

Ribosomal RNA (rRNA)
A class of RNA found in the ribosomes of cells.

Ribosomes
Small cellular components composed of specialized ribosomal RNA and protein; site of protein synthesis.
See also: RNA

Risk communication
In genetics, a process in which a genetic counselor or other medical professional interprets genetic test results and advises patients of the consequences for them and their offspring.

RNA (Ribonucleic acid)
A chemical found in the nucleus and cytoplasm of cells; it plays an important role in protein synthesis and other chemical activities of the cell. The structure of RNA is similar to that of DNA. There are several classes of RNA molecules, including messenger RNA, transfer RNA, ribosomal RNA, and other small RNAs, each serving a different purpose.

S

Sanger sequencing
A widely used method of determining the order of bases in DNA.
See also: sequencing, shotgun sequencing
Satellite
A chromosomal segment that branches off from the rest of the chromosome but is still connected by a thin filament or stalk.
Scaffold
In genomic mapping, a series of contigs that are in the right order but not necessarily connected in one continuous stretch of sequence.
Segregation
The normal biological process whereby the two pieces of a chromosome pair are separated during meiosis and randomly distributed to the germ cells.
Sequence
See: base sequence
Sequence assembly
A process whereby the order of multiple sequenced DNA fragments is determined.
Sequence tagged site (STS)
Short (200 to 500 base pairs) DNA sequence that has a single occurrence in the human genome and whose location and base sequence

are known. Detectable by polymerase chain reaction, STSs are useful for localizing and orienting the mapping and sequence data reported from many different laboratories and serve as landmarks on the developing physical map of the human genome. Expressed sequence tags (ESTs) are STSs derived from cDNAs.

Sequencing
Determination of the order of nucleotides (base sequences) in a DNA or RNA molecule or the order of amino acids in a protein.

Sequencing technology
The instrumentation and procedures used to determine the order of nucleotides in DNA.

Sex chromosome
The X or Y chromosome in human beings that determines the sex of an individual. Females have two X chromosomes in diploid cells; males have an X and a Y chromosome. The sex chromosomes comprise the 23rd chromosome pair in a karyotype.
See also: autosome

Sex-linked
Traits or diseases associated with the X or Y chromosome; generally seen in males.
See also: gene, mutation, sex chromosome

Shotgun method
Sequencing method that involves randomly sequenced cloned pieces of the genome, with no foreknowledge of where the piece originally came from. This can be contrasted with "directed" strategies, in which pieces of DNA from known chromosomal locations are sequenced. Because there are advantages to both strategies, researchers use both random (or shotgun) and directed strategies in combination to sequence the human genome.
See also: library, genomic library

Single nucleotide polymorphism (SNP)
  DNA sequence variations that occur when a single nucleotide (A, T, C, or G) in the genome sequence is altered.
  See also: mutation, polymorphism, single-gene disorder

Single-gene disorder
  Hereditary disorder caused by a mutant allele of a single gene (e.g., Duchenne muscular dystrophy, retinoblastoma, sickle cell disease).
  See also: polygenic disorders

Somatic cell
  Any cell in the body except gametes and their precursors.
  See also: gamete

Somatic cell gene therapy
  Incorporating new genetic material into cells for therapeutic purposes. The new genetic material cannot be passed to offspring.
  See also: gene therapy

Somatic cell genetic mutation
  A change in the genetic structure that is neither inherited nor passed to offspring. Also called acquired mutations.
  See also: germ line genetic mutation

Southern blotting
  Transfer by absorption of DNA fragments separated in electrophoretic gels to membrane filters for detection of specific base sequences by radio-labeled complementary probes.

Spectral karyotype (SKY)
  A graphic of all an organism's chromosomes, each labeled with a different color. Useful for identifying chromosomal abnormalities.
  See also: chromosome

Splice site
  Location in the DNA sequence where RNA removes the noncoding areas to form a continuous gene transcript for translation into a protein.

Sporadic cancer
  Cancer that occurs randomly and is not inherited from parents. Caused by DNA changes in one cell that grows and divides, spreading throughout the body.
  See also: hereditary cancer

Stem cell
  Undifferentiated, primitive cells in the bone marrow that have the ability both to multiply and to differentiate into specific blood cells.

Structural genomics
  The effort to determine the 3D structures of large numbers of proteins using both experimental techniques and computer simulation

Substitution
  In genetics, a type of mutation due to replacement of one nucleotide in a DNA sequence by another nucleotide or replacement of one amino acid in a protein by another amino acid.
  See also: mutation

Suppressor gene
  A gene that can suppress the action of another gene.

Syndrome
  The group or recognizable pattern of symptoms or abnormalities that indicate a particular trait or disease.

Syngeneic
  Genetically identical members of the same species.

Synteny
  Genes occurring in the same order on chromosomes of different species.
  See also: linkage, conserved sequence

T

Tandem repeat sequences
Multiple copies of the same base sequence on a chromosome; used as markers in physical mapping.
See also: physical map

Targeted mutagenesis
Deliberate change in the genetic structure directed at a specific site on the chromosome. Used in research to determine the targeted region's function.
See also: mutation, polymorphism

Technology transfer
The process of transferring scientific findings from research laboratories to the commercial sector.

Telomerase
The enzyme that directs the replication of telomeres.

Telomere
The end of a chromosome. This specialized structure is involved in the replication and stability of linear DNA molecules.
See also: DNA replication

Teratogenic
Substances such as chemicals or radiation that cause abnormal development of a embryo.
See also: mutatgen

Thymine (T)
A nitrogenous base, one member of the base pair AT (adenine-thymine).
See also: base pair, nucleotide

Toxicogenomics
The study of how genomes respond to environmental stressors or toxicants. Combines genome-wide mRNA expression profiling with

protein expression patterns using bioinformatics to understand the role of gene-environment interactions in disease and dysfunction.

Transcription
　The synthesis of an RNA copy from a sequence of DNA (a gene); the first step in gene expression.
　See also: translation

Transcription factor
　A protein that binds to regulatory regions and helps control gene expression.

Transcriptome
　The full complement of activated genes, mRNAs, or transcripts in a particular tissue at a particular time

Transfection
　The introduction of foreign DNA into a host cell.
　See also: cloning vector, gene therapy

Transfer RNA (tRNA)
　A class of RNA having structures with triplet nucleotide sequences that are complementary to the triplet nucleotide coding sequences of mRNA. The role of tRNAs in protein synthesis is to bond with amino acids and transfer them to the ribosomes, where proteins are assembled according to the genetic code carried by mRNA.

Transformation
　A process by which the genetic material carried by an individual cell is altered by incorporation of exogenous DNA into its genome.

Transgenic
　An experimentally produced organism in which DNA has been artificially introduced and incorporated into the organism's germ line.
　See also: cell, DNA, gene, nucleus, germ line

Translation
　The process in which the genetic code carried by mRNA directs the synthesis of proteins from amino acids.

See also: transcription

Translocation
A mutation in which a large segment of one chromosome breaks off and attaches to another chromosome.
See also: mutation

Transposable element
A class of DNA sequences that can move from one chromosomal site to another.

Trisomy
Possessing three copies of a particular chromosome instead of the normal two copies.
See also: cell, gene, gene expression, chromosome

U

Uracil
A nitrogenous base normally found in RNA but not DNA; uracil is capable of forming a base pair with adenine.
See also: base pair, nucleotide

V

Vector
See: cloning vector

Virus
A noncellular biological entity that can reproduce only within a host cell. Viruses consist of nucleic acid covered by protein; some animal viruses are also surrounded by membrane. Inside the infected cell, the virus uses the synthetic capability of the host to produce progeny virus.
See also: cloning vector

W

Western blot
A technique used to identify and locate proteins based on their ability to bind to specific antibodies.
See also: DNA, Northern blot, protein, RNA, Southern blotting
Wild type
The form of an organism that occurs most frequently in nature.
Working Draft DNA Sequence
See: Draft DNA Sequence

X

X chromosome
One of the two sex chromosomes, X and Y.
See also: Y chromosome, sex chromosome
Xenograft
Tissue or organs from an individual of one species transplanted into or grafted onto an organism of another species, genus, or family. A common example is the use of pig heart valves in humans.

Y

Y chromosome
One of the two sex chromosomes, X and Y.
See also: X chromosome, sex chromosome
Yeast artificial chromosome (YAC)
Constructed from yeast DNA, it is a vector used to clone large DNA fragments.
See also: cloning vector, cosmid

Z

Zinc-finger protein
A secondary feature of some proteins containing a zinc atom; a DNA-binding protein.
Updated 12-Oct-02

The online presentation of this publication is a special feature of the Human Genome Project Information Web site. This document may be cited in the following style:
Human Genome Program, U.S. Department of Energy, *Genomics and Its Impact on Medicine and Society: A 2001 Primer*, 2001.

For printed copies, please contact Laura Yust at Oak Ridge National Laboratory. Send questions or comments to the author, Denise K. Casey. Site designed by Marissa Mills.

APPENDIX A

Name Frequency in the US

(Reprinted with permission from the *U.S. Census Bureau, Population Division*)
How Frequently Do Names Appear?
NOTE: No specific individual information is given

See the US Census Bureau Web site at:
http://www.census.gov/genealogy/names/

For example:
US Census Bureau, 1990

(1). A "Name"
(2). Frequency in percent
(3). Cumulative Frequency in percent
(4). Rank

In the file (dist.all.last) one entry appears as:

      MOORE   0.312   5.312   9

In our Search Area sample, MOORE ranks 9th in terms of frequency. 5.312 percent of the sample population is covered by MOORE and the 8 names occurring more frequently than MOORE. The surname, MOORE, is possessed by 0.312 percent of our population sample.
<u>Detailed Methodology</u>

Variables in Names Files:
  name
  freq=Frequency in percent
  cum.freq=Cumulative Frequency in percent
  rank

First ten entries in dist.all.last

name	freq	cum.freq	rank
SMITH	1.006	1.006	1
JOHNSON	0.810	1.816	2
WILLIAMS	0.699	2.515	3
JONES	0.621	3.136	4
BROWN	0.621	3.757	5
DAVIS	0.480	4.237	6
MILLER	0.424	4.660	7
WILSON	0.339	5.000	8
MOORE	0.312	5.312	9
TAYLOR	0.311	5.623	10

First ten entries in dist.female.first

name	freq	cum.freq	rank
MARY	2.629	2.629	1
PATRICIA	1.073	3.702	2
LINDA	1.035	4.736	3
BARBARA	0.980	5.716	4

ELIZABETH	0.937	6.653	5
JENNIFER	0.932	7.586	6
MARIA	0.828	8.414	7
SUSAN	0.794	9.209	8
MARGARET	0.768	9.976	9
DOROTHY	0.727	10.703	10

First ten entries in dist.male.first

name	freq	cum.freq	rank
JAMES	3.318	3.318	1
JOHN	3.271	6.589	2
ROBERT	3.143	9.732	3
MICHAEL	2.629	12.361	4
WILLIAM	2.451	14.812	5
DAVID	2.363	17.176	6
RICHARD	1.703	18.878	7
CHARLES	1.523	20.401	8
JOSEPH	1.404	21.805	9
THOMAS	1.380	23.185	10

Source: U.S. Census Bureau, Population Division,
Population Analysis & Evaluation Staff
Maintained By: Laura K. Yax (Population Division)
Last Revised: December 20, 1999 at 11:33:07 AM

APPENDIX B:

Ethnic Genealogy Web Sites:

Acadian/Cajun http://www.acadian.org/tidbits.html
& French Canadian
African-American: http://www.cyndislist.com/african.htm
African Royalty Genealogy: http://www.uq.net.au/~zzhsoszy/
Armenian Genealogy: http://www.geocities.com/Paris/Palais/2230/
Or: http://www.feefhs.org/am/gfa.html
http://www.distantcousin.com/Links/Ethnic/Armenia/
Armenian Jews, 15th century
http://www.ubalt.edu/kulanu/nosonov.html
Asia and the Pacific: http://www.cyndislist.com/asia.htm
Austria-Hungary Empire: http://feefhs.org/ah/indexah.html
Croatia Genealogy Cross Index
http://feefhs.org/cro/indexcro.html
Or: http://feefhs.org/cro/cghs-gcg.html
Eastern Europe: http://www.cyndislist.com/easteuro.htm
Eastern European Genealogical Society, Inc.:
http://feefhs.org/ca/frg-eegs.html
Egyptian Genealogy http://www.daddezio.com/egypgen.html
Egyptian Royal Genealogy:
http://www.geocities.com/christopherjbennett/
Ethnic, Religious, and National Index 14 countries:
http://feefhs.org/ethnic.html
German Genealogical Digest: http://feefhs.org/pub/frg-ggdp.html
Greek Genealogy Sources on the Internet:
http://www-personal.umich.edu/~cgaunt/greece.html

Genealogy Societies Online List:
http://www.daddezio.com/catalog/grkndx04.html
Greek Genealogy (Hellenes-Diaspora Greek Genealogy):
 http://www.geocities.com/SouthBeach/Cove/4537/
Gypsy (Rom) Genealogy: http://www.pe.net/~kathys/gypsy.htm
Irish Travellers: http://www.pitt.edu/~alkst3/Traveller.html
Jewish Genealogy: http://www.jewishgen.org/infofiles/
Jewish-Sephardic Genealogy Sources:
http://www.orthohelp.com/geneal/sefardim.htm#TOC
Melungeon: http://www.geocities.com/Paris/5121/melungeon.htm
Native American: http://www.cyndislist.com/native.htm
Polish Genealogical Society of America:
http://feefhs.org/pol/frg-pgsa.html
Quebec and Francophone
http://www.francogene.com/quebec/amerin.html
Syrian and Lebanese Genealogy:
http://www.genealogytoday.com/family/syrian/
Unique Peoples: http://www.cyndislist.com/peoples.htm

- The Unique People's list includes:
- Black Dutch
- Doukhobors
- Gypsy, Romani, Romany & Travellers
- Melungeons
- Metis
- Miscellaneous
- Wends/Sorbs

Genealogy, (General):

Ancestry.com: http://www.ancestry.com/main.htm?lfl=m

Cyndi's List of Genealogy on the Internet: http://www.cyndislist.com/
Cyndi's List is a categorized & cross-referenced index to genealogical resources on the Internet with thousands of links.
DistantCousin.com (Uniting Cousins Worldwide)
http://distantcousin.com/Links/surname.html
Ellis Island Online: http://www.ellisisland.org/
Family History Library: http://www.familysearch.org/Eng/default.asp
http://www.familysearch.org/Eng/Search/frameset_search.asp
(The Church of Jesus Christ of Latter Day Saints) International Genealogical Index
Female Ancestors: http://www.cyndislist.com/female.htm
Genealogist's Index to the Web:
http://www.genealogytoday.com/GIWWW/?
Genealogy Web http://www.genealogyweb.com/
Genealogy Authors and Speakers: http://feefhs.org/frg/frg-a&l.html
Genealogy Today: http://www.genealogytoday.com/
My Genealogy.com http://www.genealogy.com/cgi-bin/my_main.cgi
Scriver, Dr. Charles: The Canadian Medical Hall of Fame
http://www.virtualmuseum.ca/Exhibitions/Medicentre/en/scri_print.htm
Surname Sites: http://www.cyndislist.com/surn-gen.htm
National Genealogical Society:
http://www.ngsgenealogy.org/index.htm
United States List of Local by State Genealogical Societies:
http://www.daddezio.com/society/hill/index.html
United States Vital Records List:
http://www.daddezio.com/records/room/index.html or
http://www.cyndislist.com/usvital.htm

*   *   *

APPENDIX C:

Bibliography 1: Genealogy.

A Bintel Brief: Sixty Years of Letters From the Lower East Side to the Jewish Daily Forward. Metzker, Isaac, ed Doubleday and Co. 1971. Garden City, NY

Celebrating the Family published by Ancestry.com Publishing http://shops.ancestry.com/product.asp?productid=2625&shopid=128

Climbing Your Family Tree: Online and Offline Genealogy for Kids IRA Wolfman, Tim Robinson (Illustrator), Alex Haley (Introduction) / Paperback / Workman Publishing Company, Inc. / October 2001

Complete Beginner's Guide to Genealogy, the Internet, and Your Genealogy Computer Program Karen Clifford / Paperback / Genealogical Publishing Company, Incorporated / February 2001

Complete Idiot's Guide(R) to Online Geneology Rhonda McClure / Paperback / Pearson Education / January 2002

Creating Your Family Heritage Scrapbook : From Ancestors to Grandchildren, Your Complete Resource & Idea Book for Creating a Treasured Heirloom. Nerius, Maria Given, Bill Gardner ISBN: 0761530142 Published by Prima Publishing, Aug 2001

Cyndi's List: A Comprehensive List of 70,000 Genealogy Sites on the Internet (Vol. 1 & 2) Cyndi Howells / Paperback / Genealogical Publishing Company, Incorporated / June 2001.

<u>Discovering Your Female Ancestors: Special strategies for uncovering your hard-to-find information about your female lineage.</u> Carmack, Sharon DeBartolo. Conference Lecture on Audio Tape: Carmack, Sharon DeBartolo.

<u>Folklife and Fieldwork: A Layman's Introduction to Field Techniques.</u> Bartis, Peter. Washington, DC: Library of Congress, 1990.

<u>Genealogy Online for Dummies</u> Matthew L. Helm, April Leigh Helm, April Leigh Helm, Matthew L. Helm / Paperback / Wiley, John & Sons, Incorporated / February 2001

<u>Genealogy Online</u> Elizabeth Powell Crowe / Paperback / McGraw-Hill Companies, November 2001

<u>History From Below: How to Uncover and Tell the Story of Your Community, Association, or Union.</u> Brecher, Jeremy. New Haven: Advocate Press/Commonwork Pamphlets, 1988.

<u>My Family Tree Workbook: Genealogy for Beginners</u> Rosemary A. Chorzempa / Paperback / Dover Publications, Incorporated /

<u>National Genealogical Society Quarterly</u> 79, no. 3 (September 19991): 183-93

"<u>Numbering Your Genealogy: Sound and Simple Systems.</u>" Curran, Joan Ferris.

<u>Oral History and the Law.</u> Neuenschwander, John. Pamphlet Series #1. Albuquerque: Oral History Association, 1993.

<u>Oral History for the Local Historical Society</u>. Baum, Willa K. Nashville: American Association for State and Local History, 1987.

<u>Scrapbook Storytelling</u>: Save Family Stories & Memories with Photos, Journaling & Your Own Creativity Slan, Joanna Campbell, Published by EFG, Incorporated, ISBN: 0963022288 May 1999

"The Silent Woman: Bringing a Name to Life." NE-59. Boston, MA: New England Historic Genealogical Society Sesquicentennial Conference, 1995.

The Source: A Guidebook of American Genealogy Alice Eichholz, Loretto Dennis Szucs (Editor), Sandra Hargreaves Luebking (Editor), Sandra Hargreaves Luebking (Editor) / Hardcover / MyFamily.com, Incorporated / February 1997

To Our Children's Children: Journal of Family Members, Bob Greene, D. G. Fulford 240pp. ISBN: 038549064X Publisher: Doubleday & Company, Incorporated: October 1998.

Transcribing and Editing Oral History. Nashville: American Association for State and Local History, 1991.

Using Oral History in Community History Projects. Buckendorf, Madeline, and Laurie Mercier. Pamphlet Series #4. Albuqueque: Oral History Association, 1992.

Unpuzzling Your Past: The Best-Selling Basic Guide to Genealogy (Expanded, Updated and Revised) Emily Anne Croom, Emily Croom / Paperback / F & W Publications, Incorporated / August 2001

Writing a Woman's Life. Heilbrun, Carolyn G. New York: W.W. Norton, 1988

Your Guide to the Family History Library: How to Access the World's Largest Genealogy Resource Paula Stuart Warren, James W. Warren / Paperback / F & W Publications, Incorporated / August 2001

Your Story: A Guided Interview Through Your Personal and Family History, 2nd ed., 64pp. ISBN: 0966604105 Publisher: Stack Resources, LLC

Bibliography 2:
DNA Testing and Genetics.

A Biologist's Guide to Analysis of DNA Microarray Data Steen Knudsen / Hardcover / Wiley, John & Sons, Incorporated / April 2002

Advances and Opportunities in DNA Testing and Gene Probes Business Communications Company Incorporated (Editor) / Hardcover / Business Communications / September 1996

African Exodus, The Origins of Modern Humanity Stringer, Christopher and Robin McKie. Henry Holt And Company 1997

An A to Z of DNA Science: What Scientists Mean when They Talk about Genes and Genomes Jeffre L. Witherly, Galen P. Perry, Darryl L. Leja / Paperback / Cold Spring Harbor Laboratory Press / September 2002

An Introduction to Forensic DNA Analysis Norah Rudin, Keith Inman / Hardcover / CRC Press / December 2001

Archaeogenetics: DNA and the population prehistory of Europe, Ed. Colin Renfrew & Katie Boyle. McDonald Institute Monographs. Cambridge, UK, Distributed by Oxbow Books UK. In USA: The David Brown Book Company, Oakville, CT. 2000

Cartoon Guide to Genetics Gonick, Larry, With Mark Wheelis: Paperback / HarperInformation / July 1991

DNA Detectives, The—Working Against Time, novel, Hart, Anne. Mystery and Suspense Press, iniverse.com paperback 248 pages at http://www.iuniverse.com or 1-877-823-9235.

DNA for Family Historians (ISBN 0-9539171-0-X). Savin, Alan of Maidenhead, England, is author of the 32-page book. See the Web site: http://www.savin.org/dna/dna-book.html

DNA Microarrays and Gene Expression Pierre Baldi, G. Wesley Hatfield, G. Wesley Hatfield / Hardcover / Cambridge University Press / August 2002

Microarrays for an Integrative Genomics Isaac S. Kohane, Alvin Kho, Atul J. Butte / Hardcover / MIT Press / August 2002

Does It Run in the Family?: A Consumers Guide to DNA Testing for Genetic Disorders Doris Teichler Zallen, Doris Teichler-Zallen, Doris Teichler Zallen / Hardcover / Rutgers University Press / May 1997

Double Helix, The: A Personal Account of the Discovery of the Structure of DNA James D. Watson / Paperback / Simon & Schuster Trade Paperbacks / June 2001

Genes, Peoples, and Languages Luigi Luca Cavalli-Sforza, Mark Seielstad (Translator).

Genetic Diversity Among Jews: Diseases and Markers at the DNA Level. Bonné-Tamir, B. and Adam, A. Oxford University Press. 1992.

Genetic Witness: Forensic Uses of DNA Tests DIANE Publishing Company (Editor) / Paperback / DIANE Publishing Company / April 1993

History and Geography of Human Genes, The [ABRIDGED] L. Luca Cavalli-Sforza, Paolo Menozzi (Contributor), Alberto Piazza (Contributor).

How to DNA Test Our Family Relationships Terry Carmichael, Alexander Ivanof Kuklin, Ed Grotjan / Paperback / Acen Press / November 2000

Introduction to Genetic Analysis Anthony J. Griffiths, Suzuki, Lewontin, Gelbart, David T. Suzuki, Richard C. Lewontin, Willi Gelbart,

Miller, Jeffrey H. Miller / Hardcover / W. H. Freeman Company / February 2000

Jefferson's Children: The Story of One American Family Shannon Lanier, Jane Feldman, Lucian K. Truscott (Introduction) / Hardcover / Random House Books for Young Readers / September 2000

Medical Genetics Lynn B. B. Jorde, Michael J. Bamshad, Raymond L. White, Michael J. Bamshad, John C. Carey, John C. Carey, Raymond L. White, John C. Carey / Paperback / Mosby-Year Book, Inc. / July 2000

Molecule Hunt, The: Archaeology and the Search for Ancient DNA Martin Jones / Hardcover / Arcade / April 2002

More Chemistry and Crime: From Marsh Arsenic Test to DNA Profile Richard Saferstein, Samuel M. Gerber (Editor) / Hardcover / American Chemical Society / August 1998

1996, Quest For Perfection—The Drive to Breed Better Human Beings, Maranto, Gina. Scribner, 1996

Our Molecular Future: How Nanotechnology, Robotics, Genetics, and Artificial Intelligence Will Transform Our World Mulhall, Douglas./ Hardcover / Prometheus Books / March 2002

Paternity—Disputed, Typing, PCR and DNA Tests: Index of New Information Dexter Z. Franklin / Hardcover / Abbe Pub Assn of Washington Dc / January 1998

Paternity in Primates: Tests and Theories R. D. Martin (Editor), A. F. Dickson (Editor), E. J. Wickings (Editor) / Hardcover / Karger, S Publishers / December 1991

Queen Victoria's Gene: Hemophilia and the Royal Family (Pbk) D. M. Potts, W. T. Potts / Paperback / Sutton Publishing, Limited / June 1999

Redesigning Humans: Our Inevitable Genetic Future Stock, Gregory. / Hardcover / Houghton Mifflin Company / April 2002

Rosalind Franklin: The Dark Lady of DNA, Brenda Maddox / Hardcover / HarperCollins Publishers / October 2002

Schaum's Outline Of Genetics Susan Elrod, William D. Stansfield / Paperback / McGraw-Hill Companies, The / December 2001

Seven Daughters of Eve, The: The Science That Reveals Our Genetic Ancestry. Sykes, Bryan. **ISBN:** 0393323145 **Publisher:** Norton, W. W. & Company, Inc. May 2002

Stedman's OB-GYN & Genetics Words Ellen Atwood (Editor), Stedmans / Paperback / Lippincott Williams & Wilkins / December 2000

* * *

APPENDIX D

Permissions:

Dear Anne,

You have permission to use the primer text and the photo of the DNA molecule for your book on DNA testing for genealogists. Please prominently credit the U.S. Department of Energy Human Genome Program as the source for both and also include our website for more information on the Human Genome Project and its applications: www.ornl.gov/hgmis. Yes, you can use the *Dictionary of Genetic Terms* at the end of the online version of the Primer. Please provide source citations when you use each part of the document. We would appreciate having a copy of your book when it is completed.
Sincerely,
Denise Casey

Denise K. Casey
Science Writer/Editor
Human Genome News
Human Genome Management Information System
Oak Ridge National Laboratory
1060 Commerce Park, MS 6480
Oak Ridge, TN 37830
865/574-0597; Fax: 865/574-9888; Email: caseydk@ornl.gov
HGMIS World Wide Web URL: http://www.ornl.gov/hgmis
Sponsor: U.S. Department of Energy

Harry Ostrer, M.D.
Professor of Pediatrics, Pathology, and Medicine
Director, Human Genetics Program
New York University School of Medicine
550 First Avenue, MSB 136
New York, NY 10016
tel 212 263-7596
fax 212 263-3477
email harry.ostrer@med.nyu.edu

*Have a Personal or Family History of Cancer? Consider Joining the Cancer Genetics Network

    The text of National Cancer Institute (NCI) material is in the public domain when the content was written by a government employee. Such content is not subject to copyright restrictions. One does not need special permission to reproduce or translate written text created by NCI staff. However, we would appreciate a credit line and a copy of any translated material.
    Likewise, permission is not needed to link to NCI Web sites. If you wish to use material on NCI Web sites, we strongly suggest linking directly to that information to be sure that you have the most up-to-date version.

*   *   *

INDEX

Allele, 16, 46, 151, 156, 170-171, 183, 188, 214
AncestryByDNA, 45-46, 64-66, 137-138
Ancestry.com, 6, 39, 226, 229
Appendix A, 221
    Name Frequency in the US, 221
Appendix B, 225
    Ethnic Genealogy Web Sites, 225
    Genealogy, general, 226
Appendix C, 229
    Bibliography 1, Genealogy, 229
    Bibliography 2, DNA Testing and Genetics, 231
Appendix D, 237
    Permissions, 237
Archaeogenetics, 26, 55, 153, 159, 232
Ashkenazi, 34, 47-48
Austin, John, 73
Barbujani, Guido, 26
BioGeographical Ancestry, 64, 66
Bioinformatics, 24, 50, 159, 171, 174, 179, 190, 195, 217
BRCA1 and BRCA2, 163
Cambridge Reference Sequence (CRS), 53, 62, 63
Cancer Genetics Network (CGN) (The), 160, 163, 169
Cells, 18-20, 29-30, 45, 76-78, 157-158, 172-173, 175-178, 181, 184, 186-187, 189-192, 195, 199-200, 203-204, 208, 211-215
CGAT, The DNA Code, 53
Chandler, John F, 44
City Directories, 31-32, 39, 45, 68, 120
Computational biology, 179
Craycraft Surname Project, 71

Diamond, Stanley M., 6
Dictionary of Genetic Terms, 170, 237
Diploid, 76, 173, 181, 192-193, 199, 213
Division of Cancer Control and Population Sciences (DCCPS), 160
DNA, 8, 10, 12-20, 22-42, 44-58, 60-74, 76-78, 81-82, 84, 86-90, 92-96, 98, 100, 102, 104, 106-108, 110, 112, 114, 116, 118, 120-122, 124-128, 130, 132, 134-138, 140-147, 149-150, 152, 154-159, 162, 164, 166, 168, 171-219, 222, 226, 230-234, 237-238, 240, 242
DNA Detectives (The), 50, 232
DNA for Family Historians, 36, 232
DNA testing, 3, 12-15, 18-19, 24-25, 29, 31-40, 44-45, 47, 50-51, 53, 62-63, 65-67, 69-71, 73, 77, 106-107, 120-121, 125, 135, 137, 141-143, 145-147, 159, 231, 233, 237
Demography, 6, 23, 159
Epidemiology and Genetics Research Program (EGRP), 160
Ethnic Genealogy Web Sites, 225
Family history, 4, 6, 8-10, 12, 14, 16, 18, 20, 22, 24-36, 38, 40, 42-43, 46, 48, 50, 52, 54, 56, 58, 60, 62, 64, 66, 68, 70, 72, 74, 77-78, 82, 84, 88, 90, 94, 96, 98, 100, 102, 104, 106, 108, 110, 112, 114, 116, 118, 120-122, 124, 126, 128, 130-132, 134, 136, 138, 140-142, 144-147, 150, 152, 154, 156, 158, 160, 162-164, 166, 168, 172, 174, 176, 178, 180, 182, 184, 186, 188, 190, 192, 194, 196, 198, 200, 202, 204, 206, 208, 210, 212, 214, 216, 218, 222, 226-227, 230-232, 234, 238, 240, 242
Family historians, 12, 24, 32, 36, 39, 69, 232
FamilyTreeDNA, 71, 74, 137-138, 143, 145, 150
Forensic DNA testing, 232
Frudakis, Tony, PhD, 64
Genealogy, 3, 7, 10, 12-14, 16-18, 21, 23-25, 33-40, 42-44, 51, 54, 62, 67-69, 71-72, 74, 99, 110, 120-121, 125, 131-132, 134-135, 137, 139-143, 145-146, 148-149, 159, 221, 225-227, 229-231

GENEALOGY-DNA-D-request@rootsweb.com, 35
Genetics Program New York University School of Medicine, 34, 238
Genome, 11, 24-27, 29-31, 40, 46, 51, 64-67, 76-81, 86-89, 91-92, 97, 138, 155-157, 159, 173, 176-178, 181, 183-184, 186, 190-191, 194, 197, 200, 204, 206, 208, 210, 212-214, 217, 220, 237
Genomics, 45, 54, 64-65, 77-78, 80, 86, 92-93, 97, 137-138, 170, 178, 187, 191, 215, 220, 232
GeneTree DNA Testing Center, 69-71
Haplogroup, 22-23, 41-42, 50, 53-56, 59-62, 67, 152-156
Haplotype, 14, 16-17, 21, 145-146, 152, 156, 192
High resolution, 47, 56, 61, 64
Human Genome Management Information System, 77, 237
Human Genome News, 237
Human Genome Program, 77-78, 194, 220, 237
Human Genome Project Goals, 80
Human Genome Sequence, 80, 86
HVS-1, 41, 47, 54-55, 58, 63-64, 67
HVS-2, 47, 56, 61-64, 67
Informatics and Information Technology Group, (CGN), 169
Institute of Molecular and Cell Biology, Tartu, Estonia, 40
Khait, Barbara, 6
Low resolution, 47, 67
Macaulay, Victor, 54, 55, 62, 63
MadSci.ORG, 76
Marks, Jonathan, 28
Medical history, 25
Melton, Terry, 38
Mitochondria, 30, 45, 76, 153, 157-158, 180, 200
Mitotyping Technologies, LLC., 38
Molecular genetics, 12, 23, 25-26, 34, 50, 87, 159, 201
MtDNA, 13-15, 19, 22-23, 30, 32, 36, 38-42, 44-47, 51, 53-57, 60-62, 64, 66-70, 76, 152-158

Mutations, 5, 14, 17, 22, 25, 40-41, 53-54, 56, 62-63, 90, 94, 145-146, 152, 154-156, 180-182, 208, 214
National Cancer Institute (NCI), 160, 163, 169, 238
National Center for Health Statistics in Hyattsville, 68
Nature Reviews/Genetics, 34
Neolithic, 52, 60, 159
The Network, 160, 161, 242
Oak Ridge National Laboratory, 77, 220, 237
Olson, Steve, 1, 153, 158
Onomastics, 23
Oral histories, 24, 34-35, 106-108, 110, 124, 126, 131
Ostrer, Harry M.D,, 33-34, 238
Oxford Ancestors, 2, 42, 53, 56-59, 62-64
Perego, Ugo, 12, 18
Phenomics, 10, 23-24, 44, 65, 67, 134, 142, 159
Pilot studies, 162
Population genetics, 11, 27, 207
Prosopography, 4-5, 23
Reed, Peter, 19, 42
Renfrew, Colin, 55, 153, 232
Richards, Martin, 57
Rice, Marjorie, 39
Roper Surname Project, 73
Savin, Alan, 232
Schildkraut, Joellen, 161
Science, 2-3, 23-24, 34, 36-38, 50, 69, 76-77, 86-87, 108, 159, 174, 232, 234, 237
Scriver, Dr. Charles, 227
Sequences, 1, 25-26, 31, 33, 35-36, 42, 46-47, 53-56, 58, 63, 66-68, 78, 88-91, 93, 98, 152, 156, 175, 178, 182, 187-188, 193, 202, 206, 210, 213-214, 216-218
Sequence variation, 90

Sequencing technology, 213
Sethi, Ricky J., 76
Single Nucleotide Polymorphisms (SNPs), 57, 90
SNP Consortium, 82
Sykes, Bryan, 234
Tangled Roots? Genetics Meets Genealogy, 37
Transitions, 25, 53, 63
Underhill, Peter, 38
US Census, 32, 67, 139-140, 221
U.S. Department of Energy, 77-78, 80, 220, 237
Villems, Richard, 40-41
Winn, Deborah, PhD, 160
Y-Chromosome, 13-16, 19, 22, 27, 31, 69-70, 156

* * *

Below is a list of published paperback books by Anne Hart.

Two novels are published by www.1stbooks.com and 28 or 29 books published by www.iuniverse.com. I have the audio rights only on all books published by www.iuniverse.com. I was told by 1stbooks.com that I have all rights. Always check with them to make sure as they may change and not tell me, etc.

Anne Hart

1. How to Interpret Your DNA Test Results For Family History & Ancestry
ISBN: 0-595-26334-8—Paperback—List Price: $19.95
Writers Club Press, iUniverse, Inc. Published Date: Dec. 2002
Author: Anne Hart

2. The DNA Detectives—Working Against Time (novel)
IBSN: 0-595-25339-3—Paperback—List Price $16.95
Mystery@Suspense Press, iUniverse, Inc. Published Date: Oct. 2002
Author: Anne Hart

3. Anne Joan Levine, Private Eye
ISBN: 0595218601—Paperback—List Price: $16.95
Publisher: iUniverse, Incorporated—Published Date: 03/01/2002
Author: Anne Hart

4. Astronauts and Their Cats
ISBN: 0595223303—Paperback—List Price: $11.95
Publisher: iUniverse, Incorporated—Published Date: 04/01/2002

Author: Anne Hart

5. Cleopatra's Daughter
ISBN: 0595220215—Paperback—List Price: $11.95
Publisher: iUniverse, Incorporated—Published Date: 03/01/2002
Author: Anne Hart

6. Counseling Anarchists
ISBN: 0595220541—Paperback—List Price: $14.95
Publisher: iUniverse, Incorporated—Published Date: 03/01/2002
Author: Anne Hart

7. Courage to be Jewish & the Wife of an Arab Sheik
ISBN: 0595187900—Paperback—List Price: $21.95
Publisher: iUniverse, Incorporated—Published Date: 06/01/2001
Author: Anne Hart

8. Cyber Snoop Nation
ISBN: 0595220339—Paperback—List Price: $13.95
Publisher: iUniverse, Incorporated—Published Date: 03/01/2002
Author: Anne Hart

9. Cyberscribes 1:The New Journalists (out of print)
ISBN: 1880663651—Paperback—List Price: $24.95
Publisher: Ellipsys International Publications, Incorporated—Published Date: 05/01/1997
Author: Anne Hart
Edited by: Claire C. Arias
Illustrated by: Claire C. Arias
Edited by: Stacy Marquardt

10. Date Who Unleashed Hell

ISBN: 0595219829—Paperback—List Price: $17.95
Publisher: iUniverse, Incorporated—Published Date: 03/01/2002
Author: Anne Hart

11. Day My Whole Country Turned Jewish
ISBN: 0759663807—Paperback—List Price: $18.95
Publisher: 1stBooks Library—Published Date: 06/01/2002
Author: Anne Hart

12. Four Astronauts and a Kitten
ISBN: 0595192025—Paperback—List Price: $11.95
Publisher: iUniverse, Incorporated—Published Date: 07/01/2001
Author: Anne Hart

13. Freelance Writer's E-Publishing Guidebook
ISBN: 0595189520—Paperback—List Price: $36.95
Publisher: iUniverse, Incorporated—Published Date: 06/01/2001
Author: Anne Hart

14. How to Make Money Organizing Information
ISBN: 0595236952—Paperback—List Price: $35.95
Publisher: iUniverse, Incorporated—Published Date: 08/01/2002
Author: Anne Hart

15. How to Make Money Teaching Online with Your Camcorder and PC
ISBN: 0595221238—Paperback—List Price: $36.95
Publisher: iUniverse, Incorporated—Published Date: 03/01/2002
Author: Anne Hart

16. How to Stop Elderly Abuse
ISBN: 0595235506—Paperback—List Price: $28.95
Publisher: iUniverse, Incorporated—Published Date: 07/01/2002

Author: Anne Hart

17. How Two Yellow Labs Saved the Space Program
ISBN: 0595231810—Paperback—List Price: $11.95
Publisher: iUniverse, Incorporated—Published Date: 06/01/2002
Author: Anne Hart

18. Khazars Will Rise Again!
ISBN: 059521830X—Paperback—List Price: $15.95
Publisher: iUniverse, Incorporated—Published Date: 03/01/2002
Author: Anne Hart

19. Make Money with Your Camcorder and PC
ISBN: 0595218644—Paperback—List Price: $36.95
Publisher: iUniverse, Incorporated—Published Date: 04/01/2001
Author: Anne Hart

20. Murder in the Women's Studies Department
ISBN: 0595218598—Paperback—List Price: $16.95
Publisher: iUniverse, Incorporated—Published Date: 03/01/2002
Author: Anne Hart

21. New Afghanistan's TV Anchorwoman
ISBN: 0595215572—Paperback—List Price: $23.95
Publisher: iUniverse, Incorporated—Published Date: 02/01/2002
Author: Anne Hart

22. Power Dating Games
ISBN: 059519186X—Paperback—List Price: $23.95
Publisher: iUniverse, Incorporated—Published Date: 07/01/2001
Author: Anne Hart

23. Private Eye Called Mama Africa
ISBN: 0595189407—Paperback—List Price: $25.95
Publisher: iUniverse, Incorporated—Published Date: 06/01/2001
Author: Anne Hart

24. Sacramento Latina
ISBN: 0595220614—Paperback—List Price: $29.95
Publisher: iUniverse, Incorporated—Published Date: 03/01/2002
Author: Anne Hart

25. Tools for Mystery Writers
ISBN: 0595217478—Paperback—List Price: $28.95
Publisher: iUniverse, Incorporated—Published Date: 03/01/2002
Author: Anne Hart

26. Verbal Intercourse
ISBN: 0595219462—Paperback—List Price: $17.95
Publisher: iUniverse, Incorporated—Published Date: 03/01/2002
Author: Anne Hart

27. Winning Resumes for Computer Personnel
ISBN: 0764101307—Paperback—List Price: $12.95
Publisher: Barrons Educational Series, Incorporated—Published Date: 02/01/1998
Author: Anne Hart

28. Writer?s Bible
ISBN: 0595193056—Paperback—List Price: $28.95
Publisher: iUniverse, Incorporated—Published Date: 08/01/2001
Author: Anne Hart

29. Writing What People Buy

ISBN: 0595219365—Paperback—List Price: $24.95
Publisher: iUniverse, Incorporated—Published Date: 03/01/2002
Author: Anne Hart

30. Year My Whole Country Turned Jewish
ISBN: 0759672512—Paperback—List Price: $14.95
Publisher: 1stBooks Library—Published Date: 03/01/2002
Author: Anne Hart

0-595-26334-8

CPSIA information can be obtained at www.ICGtesting.com
Printed in the USA
LVOW11s0803161214

419038LV00001B/380/A